Seasonal Quilting

A Year in Stitches

Cheryl Fall

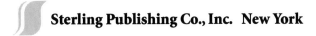 **Sterling Publishing Co., Inc. New York**

Acknowledgments

To my wonderful husband, Tony, and our daughters, Rebecca and Ashley. Thank you for your patience!

I also thank the following manufacturers and individuals for sharing their products or knowledge: Coats & Clark, Pellon, Mountain Mist, V.I.P. Fabrics, Bernina of America, Mr. R. W. Hoffman.

Photographs by Nancy Palubniak, New York City
Edited by Isabel Stein

Note: We have made every effort to ensure the accuracy and completeness of the instructions in this book. However, we cannot be responsible for human error or for the results when using materials other than those specified in the instructions, or for variations in individual work.

Library of Congress Cataloging-in-Publication Data

Fall, Cheryl C.
    Seasonal quilting: a year in stitches / Cheryl C. Fall.
    p.   cm.
    Includes index.
    ISBN 0-8069-8658-1
    1. Quilting—Patterns. 2. Appliqué—Patterns. 3. Holiday
decorations. I. Title.
TT835.F337 1993
746.46—dc20   93-25621
                                       CIP

10 9 8 7 6 5 4 3 2 1

Published by Sterling Publishing Company, Inc.
387 Park Avenue South, New York, N.Y. 10016
© 1994 by Cheryl C. Fall
Distributed in Canada by Sterling Publishing
c/o Canadian Manda Group, P.O. Box 920, Station U
Toronto, Ontario, Canada M8Z 5P9
Distributed in Great Britain and Europe by Cassell PLC
Villiers House, 41/47 Strand, London WC2N 5JE, England
Distributed in Australia by Capricorn Link Ltd.
P.O. Box 665, Lane Cove, NSW 2066
Printed and bound in Hong Kong
All rights reserved

Sterling ISBN 0-8069-8658-1

Contents

Preface

During the course of a year there are many occasions that call for a unique gift or decoration. A birthday, holiday, or even an ordinary day is made special by something handmade. This book is intended to fill your year with four seasons' worth of special projects. Many of the designs are centered around the traditional holidays such as Easter, Halloween, Thanksgiving, and Christmas, but others are for the nontraditional. These might include the birth of a new baby, opening day of the boating season, teatime with a friend, or the first day of the new school year.

All of the projects are easy to stitch and require no special equipment or tools beyond those usually found in the home sewer's workroom. All you need are a few basic materials, your time, and basic sewing skills. Enjoy your year and fill your seasons with love and handmades!

Metric Table

MM—MILLIMETRES   CM—CENTIMETRES

INCHES TO MILLIMETRES AND CENTIMETRES

INCHES	MM	CM	INCHES	CM	INCHES	CM
⅛	3	0.3	9	22.9	30	76.2
¼	6	0.6	10	25.4	31	78.7
⅜	10	1.0	11	27.9	32	81.3
½	13	1.3	12	30.5	33	83.8
⅝	16	1.6	13	33.0	34	86.4
¾	19	1.9	14	35.6	35	88.9
⅞	22	2.2	15	38.1	36	91.4
1	25	2.5	16	40.6	37	94.0
1¼	32	3.2	17	43.2	38	96.5
1½	38	3.8	18	45.7	39	99.1
1¾	44	4.4	19	48.3	40	101.6
2	51	5.1	20	50.8	41	104.1
2½	64	6.4	21	53.3	42	106.7
3	76	7.6	22	55.9	43	109.2
3½	89	8.9	23	58.4	44	111.8
4	102	10.2	24	61.0	45	114.3
4½	114	11.4	25	63.5	46	116.8
5	127	12.7	26	66.0	47	119.4
6	152	15.2	27	68.6	48	121.9
7	178	17.8	28	71.1	49	124.5
8	203	20.3	29	73.7	50	127.0

YARDS TO METRES

YARDS	METRES	YARDS	METRES	YARDS	METRES	YARDS	METRES	YARDS	METRES
⅛	0.11	2⅛	1.94	4⅛	3.77	6⅛	5.60	8⅛	7.43
¼	0.23	2¼	2.06	4¼	3.89	6¼	5.72	8¼	7.54
⅜	0.34	2⅜	2.17	4⅜	4.00	6⅜	5.83	8⅜	7.66
½	0.46	2½	2.29	4½	4.11	6½	5.94	8½	7.77
⅝	0.57	2⅝	2.40	4⅝	4.23	6⅝	6.06	8⅝	7.89
¾	0.69	2¾	2.51	4¾	4.34	6¾	6.17	8¾	8.00
⅞	0.80	2⅞	2.63	4⅞	4.46	6⅞	6.29	8⅞	8.12
1	0.91	3	2.74	5	4.57	7	6.40	9	8.23
1⅛	1.03	3⅛	2.86	5⅛	4.69	7⅛	6.52	9⅛	8.34
1¼	1.14	3¼	2.97	5¼	4.80	7¼	6.63	9¼	8.46
1⅜	1.26	3⅜	3.09	5⅜	4.91	7⅜	6.74	9⅜	8.57
1½	1.37	3½	3.20	5½	5.03	7½	6.86	9½	8.69
1⅝	1.49	3⅝	3.31	5⅝	5.14	7⅝	6.97	9⅝	8.80
1¾	1.60	3¾	3.43	5¾	5.26	7¾	7.09	9¾	8.92
1⅞	1.71	3⅞	3.54	5⅞	5.37	7⅞	7.20	9⅞	9.03
2	1.83	4	3.66	6	5.49	8	7.32	10	9.14

Getting Started

Necessary Tools

The tools required for making the projects in this book are all readily available and may be found in most home sewers' workrooms:

- *a sewing machine*

- *a good, sharp pair of scissors*

- *thimbles for hand-sewing and quilting*

- *embroidery hoop*

- *needles for both hand sewing and machine sewing, including crewel embroidery needles, sharps, and betweens (short needles of sizes 5 to 11, used for quilting)*

- *a heavy plastic ruler*

- *a pen with waterproof ink for tracing designs on paper or cardboard*

- *a blue pencil, a dressmaker's pencil, or tailor's chalk for transferring patterns to fabric (don't use regular pencil or anything permanent for this purpose. Test the pencil to be sure it won't spoil your fabric by marking and washing a fabric scrap to be sure it washes out)*

- *an iron*

- *graph paper or other gridded paper for enlarging patterns*

Other useful items are:

- *a #2 pencil*

- *a soft white eraser*

- *large sheets of paper*

- *a triangle or T-square*

- *scraps of cardboard for making templates*

- *tracing paper*

- *a rotary cutter for cutting fabrics (available at most fabric stores)*

- *a self-healing cutting board for use with a rotary cutter*

Symbols and Abbreviations

The following symbols and abbreviations are used throughout the book:

- RS   right side of fabric

- WS   wrong side of fabric

- ↕   place on grainline or parallel to the finished edge of the fabric (the selvage)

- (R)   indicates a pattern piece that is traced and reversed before being cut out

Materials

The materials used in this book are common ones. All the fabrics I used were 44"-wide 100% cotton fabrics; the yardages are based on this width. Prewash and press all fabrics before cutting to avoid their shrinkage in a completed project. Replace any fabrics that continue to "bleed" after they are laundered (that is, the dye continues to wash out). These are important steps; few things are as disappointing as the shrinking or bleeding after washing of a project that took a great investment of your time. Remove selvages by trimming them off before cutting your projects, as selvage areas are very difficult to quilt.

The quilt batting and craft fleece recommended for the projects are all 100% polyester; they do not need prewashing. If you choose to work with cotton batting instead, read the manufacturer's recommendations on the package, as some of them require prewashing. Quilt batting is used when a traditional weight is needed, for bed coverings or baby blankets. Fleece is needed when the project requires a bit more body and support, such as for wall hangings and place mats; however, dense, low-loft polyester quilt batting can be used in place of fleece.

The threads used are all-purpose threads, extra-strong hand-quilting threads, and rayon machine-embroidery threads. All-purpose thread may be used in place of the rayon thread. Keep in mind, however, that rayon will give a nice smooth, evenly filled finish. Do not use rayon for any assembly work, as it is a purely decorative thread. If you are a purist and prefer to use a thread made from the same material as your project, you may choose to use 100% cotton thread; however, the finished project will not hold up to repeated use and washings as well.

The embroidery floss recommended is 6-strand 100% cotton floss. Separate a piece of floss into individual strands, and use the number of strands indicated in the pattern for the embroidery. If all 6 strands are required, separate them and regroup them. This will take the twist out of the floss and will allow your stitches to lie flat.

General Directions

Enlarging a Reduced Pattern

To enlarge a pattern from a reduced drawing (Fig. 1a), first trace the pattern onto a piece of tracing paper and connect the grid lines across the pattern (Fig. 1b) with a ruler or straight edge. Label the lines as shown in Figure 1b. Using a sharp pencil and a ruler, redraw the grid on a large sheet of paper, making the grid boxes the size given in the pattern instructions. If you have already-gridded paper available, such as graph paper, you can use that. For example, if the pattern states, "one square = 1″ × 1″," draw a grid of 1″ × 1″ squares. Draw the same number of lines as there are in the reduced pattern grid. Label them as you did in the reduced pattern drawing. Place a dot on the large grid wherever a grid line intersects a pattern line on the reduced pattern. To connect the dots, place additional dots between the original group of dots you made, judging where they go by referring to the reduced pattern (see Fig. 1c, left side). Then connect the dots to form the full-size pattern (Fig. 1c, right side).

Making Templates and Tracing a Pattern

All full-size piecing patterns in this book include seam allowances of ¼″, unless otherwise noted. (Appliqué patterns are given without seam al-

lowances, however.) Make templates from the patterns using stiff paper or lightweight cardboard. Include seamlines, cutting lines, dots, and grain arrows on all templates and label them with the name or letter of the piece. If you wish, glue fine sandpaper to the backs of the templates to prevent their slipping while you trace around them. Trace around the required number of pieces on the wrong side of the appropriate fabric, using any of the fabric-marking tools mentioned in the Necessary Tools section above. Align the grainline of the fabric (the lengthwise grain) with the grainline arrows indicated on the pattern piece. Remember to reverse a pattern piece, when indicated, as follows: flip the pattern over and trace around it with its wrong side up. When only half of the pattern is given, trace the first side of the pattern, mark the centerline, flip the pattern over, and trace around the opposite side of template to make the full pattern.

Machine Piecing

Using a ¼″ seam allowance, stitch pieces together, with right sides of material facing. When stitching into the corners, *stop* at the intersection of the two lines of the seam allowances: the intersection is indicated by small dots on pattern pieces (see Fig. 2). If you are joining two pieced units with matching seamline areas, press the seam allowances to opposite sides of the seam before joining them, to distribute the fabrics evenly and to avoid fabric "lumps" in the finished product.

Hand Piecing

Follow the instructions for machine piecing, but use a "sharp" needle, size 7 or 8, and all-purpose thread. To join pieces, take short running stitches (Fig. 3), approximately 10 to 12 stitches to the inch. Backstitch to secure the ends.

Pressing

Always press your seams after stitching. To press properly, press along the seamline *before* opening out the joined pieces. After opening them, press the seam allowances towards the darker fabric

2 Machine piecing. Stop stitching at the dots indicated on the pattern pieces (or where two seamlines meet).

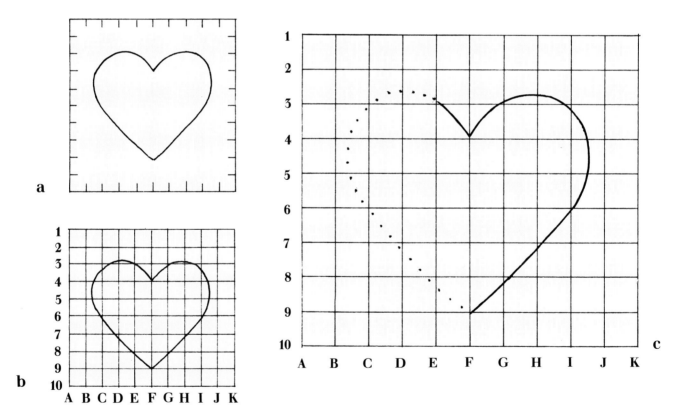

*1 Enlarging a pattern. **a:** Reduced pattern with grid lines. **b:** Traced-out pattern with completed and labelled grid lines. **c:** Large grid, labelled the same way as the small grid. First dots are made at intersections of grid; then more dots are drawn between them. They are then connected by lines.*

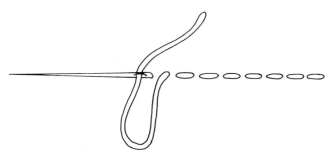

3 The running stitch, used for hand piecing.

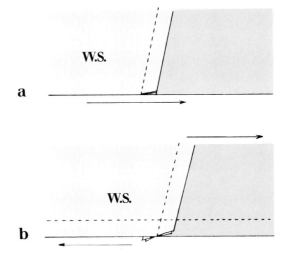

*4 Pressing of seam allowances. **a:** Press single seam allowances towards the darker fabric. **b:** Press double seam allowances in opposite directions to distribute the thickness. Use a dry iron.*

(see Fig. 4) to avoid their showing through on your completed project. Be sure to press with a *dry* iron. The use of steam or starch can stretch and distort your fabric pieces. This is important to remember when piecing must be precise and accurate, such as for the Bow-Tie Bunnies Wall Hanging.

Machine Appliqué

Many of the machine appliqué patterns in this book suggest the use of fusible webbing. Machine appliqué patterns do not need or include seam allowances on appliqué shapes. Those projects that use hand appliqué will instruct you to add the seam allowance in the directions. (Most of the machine appliqué patterns can be adapted for hand appliqué by adding ¼″ seam allowance around each appliqué pattern.) Fusible webbing with paper on one side, such as Pellon's Wonder Under,® is recommended for machine appliqué. This wonderful invention is used as follows:

1. Trace patterns onto the paper side of the webbing. Keep in mind that patterns will be facing the opposite direction after you fuse them to the fabric; therefore, you will need to reverse the patterns before tracing them on the paper side of the webbing. Do this by tracing the pattern pieces in the book onto transparent tissue or tracing paper; then turn the tissue over and trace the patterns from the wrong side onto the paper side of the webbing.

2. Cut the shapes roughly from the webbing, and fuse them in place on the wrong side of the required fabric. Cut the shapes from the

appropriate fabric, remove the paper backing from the pieces, and fuse the pieces in place on your background with a hot iron. Consult the instructions from the manufacturer of the specific webbing you have for details of this process.

3. Pin or hand-baste a stabilizer to the back side of your work. (You may also use freezer paper as a stabilizer by ironing the shiny side of the paper to the back side of your work.) *Always* be sure to use a stabilizer when doing machine appliqué, to avoid puckering. Stabilizer is available by the yard in most fabric stores, or you can use plain paper.

4. Machine appliqué the pieces in place, using a narrow machine satin stitch (approximately ⅛″ wide), preferably with rayon machine embroidery thread. All-purpose thread will also give good results. Use a neutral-colored thread in the bobbin, and use thread to match each individual appliqué piece threaded through the machine. *Loosen* the upper machine tension slightly so that none of the bobbin thread is pulled to the top of your work. If any bobbin thread still comes to the surface of your work, you may need to change your needle. Use a brand-new size 9

or 11 universal point needle. When stitching, be sure you completely cover the raw edge of the appliqué. Pivot your fabric around sharp curves, stopping the needle in the appliqué for inside curves at frequent intervals (see the inside curve of the teardrop in Fig. 5a, for example). In the base fabric, stop on the outside curve (see dots on the outside of the teardrop). When appliquéing points, the stitches should be tapered by narrowing the width of the satin stitch as you stitch into the points (see Fig. 5a). To appliqué on corners, pivot as shown in Fig. 5c. After the stitching is completed, remove the stabilizer and press your work.

Hand Appliqué

To appliqué by hand, lightly trace the appliqué pattern pieces onto the right side of the appropriate fabrics with light blue pencil or dressmaker's chalk. Appliqué patterns aren't drawn with seam allowances in this book, so add the ¼″ seam allowances around each shape as you cut it from the fabric for hand appliqué. Turn under the seam allowances, basting them down to the back of the shape itself (Fig. 6) if you wish. (For any piece that has another piece overlapping it, don't turn down the raw edge that is going to be covered over, however.) Clip the curves of the seam allowances on the appliqué pieces as necessary to make them

lie flat. Trace out the entire full-size appliqué pattern from the book onto a piece of paper. Align the entire pattern under the background fabric on which the pieces will be appliquéd. Tape the pattern and the fabric to your work surface and *lightly* trace the outlines of each appliqué piece onto the background fabric with light blue washable coloring pencil. This tracing will serve as a positioning guide for attaching all the pieces. Also transfer any embroidery markings that go on the background fabric. Pin and baste the fabric pieces to be appliquéd to the base fabric. Appliqué the shapes in place, using thread to match the individual appliqué pieces and a good hand needle (a size 7 sharp is recommended). Take small, hidden stitches.

Hand Embroidery

For projects requiring hand embroidery, several stitches are used; they are easy to do. Separate 6-strand cotton embroidery floss into the number of strands indicated in the project. Use a size 7 or 8 crewel or embroidery needle. These needles have larger eyes than sharps or betweens, to accommodate embroidery threads, which are thicker. Do not pull your stitches too tightly as you don't want your work to pucker, and *always use an embroidery hoop* to keep an even tension on your work. The embroidery stitches used in this book are shown in Figure 7.

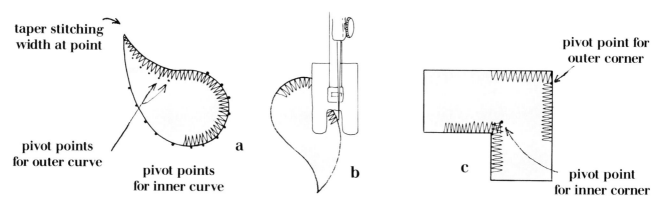

5 *Machine appliqué.* ***a:*** *Pivot your fabric around sharp curves, stopping the needle in the appliqué for inside curves at frequent intervals, and on the outside in the base fabric. Narrow the width of your satin stitch as you go into the pointed part of an appliqué.* ***b:*** *The needle is stopped on the outside edge to pivot on an outer curve. The needle is shown in the left swing of the zigzag satin stitch.* ***c:*** *Appliqué on a corner, showing pivot points.*

seam allowance

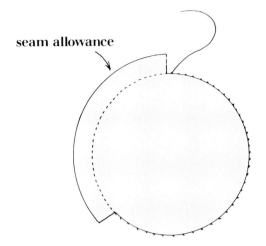

6 Hand appliqué. Fold under the seam allowances, baste them to the back of the appliqué piece if you wish, and sew the shape to the base fabric with small, hidden stitches. Appliqué patterns in this book are drawn without *seam allowances. Add ¼" seam allowance around them for hand appliqué before cutting them out.*

Applying Piping

You can use prepackaged piping for all the projects that need piping. Piping is easily applied (see Fig. 8). You can make your own piping by making bias-cut strips of material, joining them as for making bias strips (see Fig. 11b, below), folding them in half lengthwise around cord, and machine-stitching them closed near to the cord, using a zipper foot and stitching along the length. Prewash and dry the fabric and cord before you cut them if you make your own piping.

To apply piping on a straight edge, simply lay the piping along the seamline on the right side of the fabric with the raw edges of the piping even with the raw edges of the fabric, and baste the piping in place. To pipe a rectangle, baste the piping along the seamline and clip the seam allowance of the piping and the fabric at the corners, to ease turning (Fig. 8a). Do not cut through the stitching on the piping when you clip the seam allowance, however. To pipe curves, clip into the seam allowance approximately every ¼" to ½" as needed, to make the piping lie flat (Fig. 8b). Baste the piping as you would on a straight edge. To join the ends of piping when you finish surrounding a shape with it, cut the cord inside the fabric ends so that the cord ends will touch but not overlap

backstitch or stem stitch

running stitch

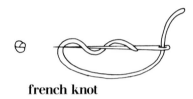

french knot

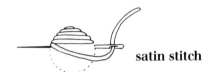

satin stitch

featherstitch

7 Hand embroidery stitches.

where they meet, but leave about ½" fabric beyond the ends of the cord. Butt the cord ends together. Fold under the raw edge of one fabric end to where the cord ends, and overlap it with the other fabric end; slipstitch the ends together.

Basting

Before you quilt, it's necessary to secure the three layers—the quilt top, batting, and backing—with

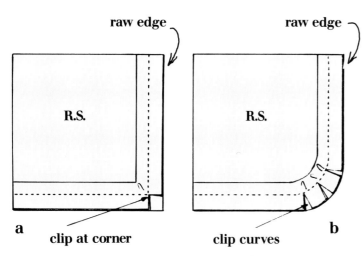

a clip at corner   clip curves **b**

*8 Applying piping. **a**: to a rectangular corner; **b**: to a curve.*

basting stitches. Hand-baste or pin-baste the quilt top to its batting and backing. (Pin-basting means pinning the layers together instead of basting them with thread.) Baste from the center out in all directions, like a spiderweb, smoothing out any wrinkles in the fabric back and front as you go.

Machine Quilting

Mark your quilting lines with masking tape, washable light blue pencil, or chalk. Start at the center of the quilt and work your way out to the sides, smoothing the fabric as tightly and evenly as possible. If your sewing machine has an even-feed or "walking-foot," this is an ideal place to use it. If not, use a straight-stitch foot and lower the feed dogs (see your machine's instruction manual if you do not know how to do this). Use a neutral-colored thread in the bobbin and clear nylon monofilament or a complementary colored thread in the top of the machine. Loosen the upper tension slightly so that none of the bobbin thread is pulled through to the right side of the work.

Slowly stitch along all seamlines, starting at the center of the quilt and working your way to the edges. Stitch around each appliqué shape, in the ditch of the seams, and along the marked quilting lines. (You may, of course, choose some other quilting pattern if you prefer.) Do not stitch quickly as you may loose control of your work. Start and end your stitching with a backstitch. Pull the thread tails from the front of the quilt to the

back side and clip them. You may also choose to bury them by threading the tails through a needle and running the needle into the batting for about 2″. Then pull the needle up and, with the thread pulled tight, clip off the excess thread tail. When you release it, the ends will be pulled under the surface.

Hand Quilting

Assemble, baste, and mark the quilt as for machine quilting. Thread a "between" needle with a length of quilting thread, and knot the end of the thread. Push the needle and thread through the top of the work, pulling the thread and the knot through the fabric and burying the knot in the batting (see the detail of the quilting stitch in Figure 9). Quilt along the seamlines, ¼″ in from the seamlines and the appliqué edges, and along the marked quilting lines, using small, closely spaced running stitches. Make sure your stitches penetrate the backing and do not simply catch in the batting. Place a finger under your work; you should feel the needle point coming through the back side. Be careful not to puncture yourself! You can protect your underneath finger by wrapping adhesive tape around it or using a finger protector, sold in quilting shops.

Applying and Making Bias Binding

You can purchase prepackaged extra-wide double-fold bias bindings for the projects in this book; however, you can make your own if you wish (see below). Use thread to match the binding when you attach it. Several sizes of binding are available, but all are applied in the same manner (see Fig. 10):

1. Unfold the binding and pin or baste the narrowest raw edge to align with the outside raw edge of the quilt top (see Fig. 10a). Stitch along the crease in the binding until you are within ¼″ of the end of the quilt. End off the thread.

2. At the corner, fold the binding up, aligning the side of the binding with the side of the quilt top (see Fig. 10b).

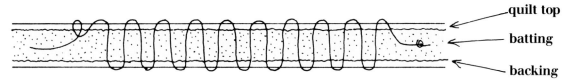

9 *Cross-section of quilt, showing hand-quilting stitch. The initial knot is pulled through and buried in the batting.*

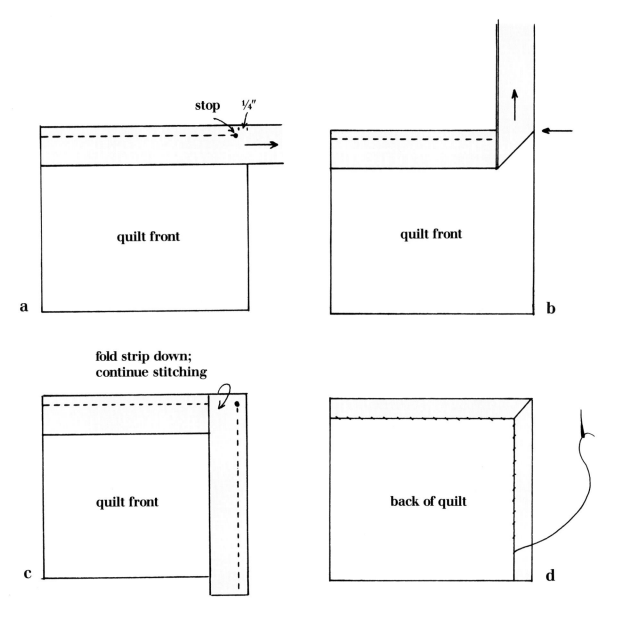

10 *Applying binding. **a:** Stitch along the crease in the binding until you are ¼" from the end of the quilt. **b:** Fold the binding strip upwards at the corner. **c:** Fold the binding strip downwards and continue stitching. **d:** Turn the loose edge of the binding to the back and hand-stitch it in place.*

3. Fold the binding down, having the top fold of the binding aligned with the top edge of the quilt (see Fig. 10c). Continue stitching.

4. Repeat the folding and stitching procedure for the rest of the sides of the quilt that need binding.

5. Fold the loose long edge of the binding to the back of the quilt along the remaining crease, turning the raw edge under. Pin the binding in place at the back of the quilt, and hand-stitch the binding in place, following the seamline (Fig. 10d); be sure that your stitches aren't visible on the quilt top.

If you prefer to make your own bias binding, cut strips of fabric on the bias (at a 45° angle to the fabric's cross grain) that are 4 times as wide as the desired finished width of the binding. Cut as many as you need for your project. Then stitch the strips together, with right sides of material facing, at the ends, using a ¼″ seam allowance (Fig. 11c). Press the seam allowances open. Trim off the "tails" where the strips are joined. To fold the bias tape, fold it first along the center of the tape and press it. Open out the tape again. Next, fold the edges of each side of the tape in to meet at the previously made center-fold line, and press the two side folds (see Fig. 11d). Fold the tape again along the center crease of the strip (Fig. 11e), and you have ready-to-use double-fold bias binding.

Hanging a Quilted Project

To hang a wall hanging or quilt, follow the steps given below:

1. Cut a strip of fabric (it could be the same fabric as your quilt back) 8″ wide and of length 1″ shorter than the top of your wall hanging. (For example, if the top is 36″, the strip would be 8″ × 35″.)

2. Fold the strip lengthwise, with right sides together, and stitch it along the long side to form a tube.

3. Turn the tube right-side out.

4. Hem each end.

5. Flatten the tube so that one long side is a fold and the other has the seamline on it. Press.

6. Center the tube length on the back of the quilt top center.

7. Sew the folded edge of the tube along the top of the quilt back with a hand slipstitch and strong thread.

8. Smooth down and attach the other long seam edge of the tube to the quilt back with slipstitching; now both long sides are attached but the ends of the tube are open.

9. Choose a dowel, rod, or flat wooden strip slightly wider than the quilt top. Put the rod or other support through the tube of material and hang the wall hanging on the wall.

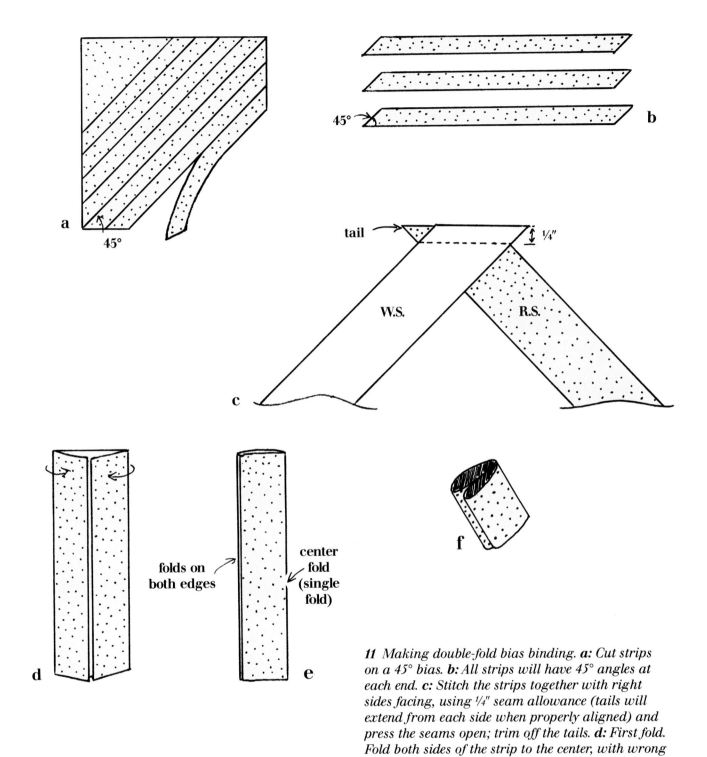

a
45°

45°
b

tail
¼"
W.S.
R.S.
c

folds on
both edges

center
fold
(single
fold)

d

e

f

11 Making double-fold bias binding. a: Cut strips on a 45° bias. b: All strips will have 45° angles at each end. c: Stitch the strips together with right sides facing, using ¼" seam allowance (tails will extend from each side when properly aligned) and press the seams open; trim off the tails. d: First fold. Fold both sides of the strip to the center, with wrong sides facing in. e: Second fold. Fold the entire strip along the center, with the already folded parts on the inside. f: End view of binding.

Spring Has Sprung

Crazy-Pieced Valentine Lap Quilt and Pillow

Surprise your sweetie with this easy-to-make set. Finished size of pillow: 12″ × 12″, excluding ruffle. Finished size of quilt: 29″ × 40″ (block size: 10″ × 10″).

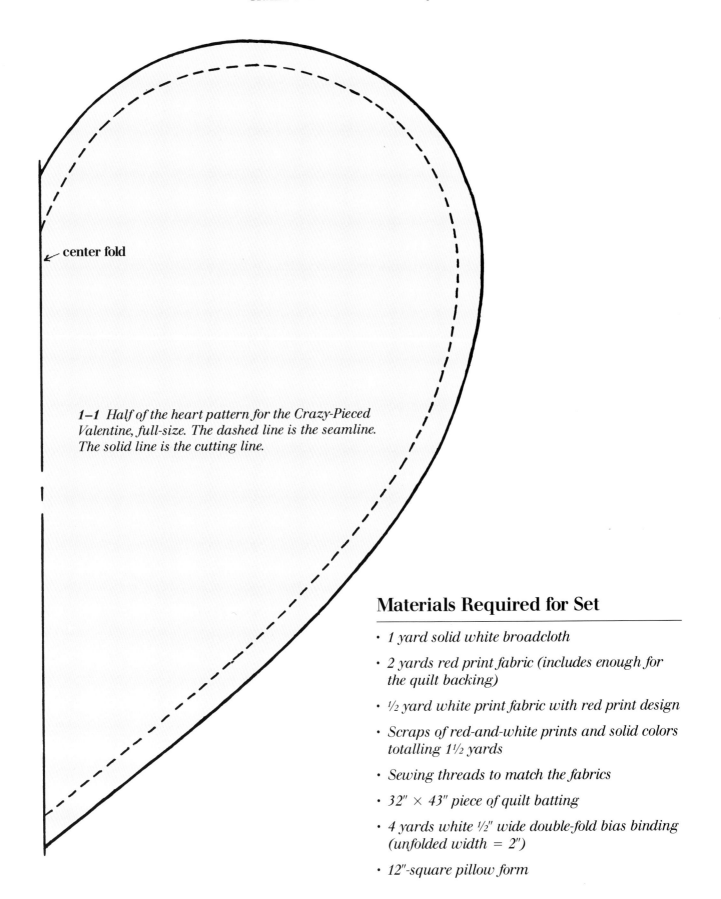

← **center fold**

1–1 Half of the heart pattern for the Crazy-Pieced Valentine, full-size. The dashed line is the seamline. The solid line is the cutting line.

Materials Required for Set

- *1 yard solid white broadcloth*
- *2 yards red print fabric (includes enough for the quilt backing)*
- *½ yard white print fabric with red print design*
- *Scraps of red-and-white prints and solid colors totalling 1½ yards*
- *Sewing threads to match the fabrics*
- *32" × 43" piece of quilt batting*
- *4 yards white ½" wide double-fold bias binding (unfolded width = 2")*
- *12"-square pillow form*

Directions for the Quilt

Note: Unless otherwise stated, given measurements include ¼″ seam allowances.

1. Using the heart template (Fig. 1–1) make a full heart pattern from paper as follows: Fold a piece of tracing paper in half lengthwise. Trace the half-heart on the right side of the folded paper, with the center of the heart on the paper's fold line. Cut out the heart through both thicknesses of paper and unfold it.

2. Cut seven 10½″ squares from solid white broadcloth. Fold each square into quarters and press them to mark the centers.

3. Tear or cut the scrap fabrics into strips and triangles no larger than 3″ wide. Stitch the scraps together, with right sides of fabric facing and ¼″ seam allowances, to form a new crazy-pieced fabric, approximately 20″ × 36″ in size. Using the heart pattern made in Step 1, cut out 6 hearts from the pieced fabric. Restitch the scraps together if necessary and cut out a seventh heart to use for the pillow. Turn the ¼″ seam allowances to the back side of each heart. Hand-appliqué one heart to the center of each white square cut in Step 2 (see photo). Press each completed block. Set one appliquéd square aside for the pillow top.

4. For the short sashing strips (A) of the quilt, cut nine 1½″ × 10½″ strips from the white print fabric.

5. Alternating strips and blocks, make a row like Row 1 in Fig. 1–2, using 2 blocks and 3 strips for each row. Piece the blocks and strips with right sides of the material facing each other, using ¼″ seam allowances.

6. Repeat Step 5 to make Row 2 and Row 3 (see Fig. 1–2).

7. Cut four 1½″ × 23½″ long sashing strips (B; see Fig. 1–2) from the same material used for the short sashing strips.

8. With the right sides of the material facing, join the long B sashing strips to the heart block rows, as shown in Figure 1–2, to make the central unit of the valentine quilt.

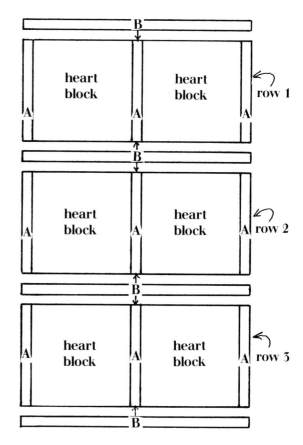

1–2 Construction diagram for Crazy-Pieced Valentine Quilt. A, short sashing strips. B, long sashing strips.

9. To make the borders, cut two 3½″ × 34½″ strips from the red print fabric and stitch them to the long sides of the central quilt unit made in Step 8.

10. Cut two 3½″ × 29½″ strips from the red heart print material, and stitch them to the top and bottom of the unit made in Step 9 (see color photo).

11. Measure your quilt top. You will need a backing and batting about 2″ longer and 2″ wider than the quilt top, or about 31″ × 42″. Cut a piece of red print fabric for the backing, about 31″ × 42″, and put it face-down on your work surface. Center the batting over the backing and center the quilt top, right-side up, over the batting. Pin and baste the three layers together.

12. Using machine or hand quilting, quilt around all the seamlines and around the

heart appliqués, or quilt in some other pattern you enjoy (see General Directions).

13. Baste around the edges of the quilt, ¼" in from the raw edges of the quilt top. Trim away the excess batting and backing, and bind the quilt with the white binding (see General Directions for binding instructions).

Directions for the Pillow

1. Take the remaining appliquéd heart block made in Step 3 of the quilt instructions. Cut two sashing strips 1½" × 10½" from the white print material and stitch them to the sides of the heart block.

2. Cut two more strips from the same material, of 1½" × 12½" size, and stitch them to the top and bottom of the unit you made in Step 1. Press.

3. For the ruffle, cut three 6½" × 44" strips from the red print material. Stitch the 3 strips together by their short ends to form a long band. Fold the band in half lengthwise, with right sides facing, aligning raw edges, to make a 44" × 3¼" rectangle. Pin the two layers of each short end together and stitch across each short end with a ¼" seam allowance to close the ends. Turn the ruffle right-side out and press it.

4. With pencil or chalk marks, mark off the length of the ruffle into 4 equal sections (Fig. 1–3). Make a ¼" cut into the seam allowance at each mark. Gather the folded ruffle on its raw edges between each cut (Fig. 1–4) with basting. Place the ruffle's cut marks at the corners of the pillow top made in Step 2, adjusting the ruffle's fullness evenly between the cut marks. Baste the ruffle to the right side of the pillow top with raw edges aligned, with a ¼" seam allowance.

5. Cut a 12½" square from any of the remaining fabrics for the pillow backing. Stitch the pillow top to the pillow backing, with right sides together and ¼" seam allowance, along 3 sides, leaving the bottom open for turning. Clip the seam allowance at the corners to ease turning and turn the pillow cover right-side out. Insert the pillow form in the cover, and stitch the opening closed.

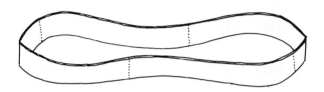

1–3 With chalk, mark lines to visually divide the folded ruffle into 4 equal parts.

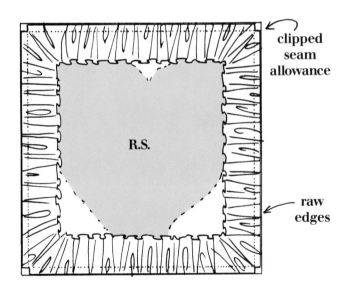

1–4 Place one mark of the strip at each corner. Clip the corners in the seam allowance and gather the ruffle between the marks. Baste the ruffle to the pillow top with raw edges aligned.

Bow-Tie Bunnies Wall Hanging

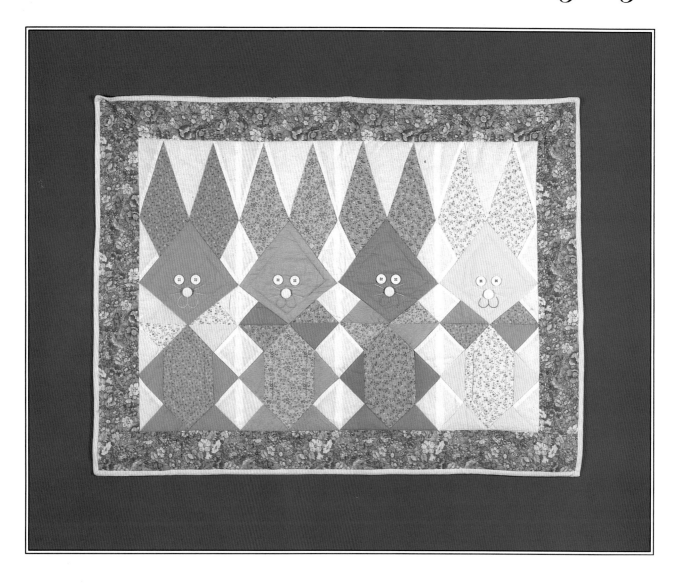

These cheery little bunnies are sure to brighten up even the rainiest of Easters! Finished size of wall hanging: 28″ × 38″ (finished block size: 8″ × 22″).

Materials Required

- *¼ yard* each *of pastel blue, pink, yellow, and green solid-color fabric*
- *¼ yard* each *of blue, pink, yellow, and green calico prints*
- *½ yard* each *of white solid broadcloth and multicolored floral print*
- *1 yard fabric of your choice for the quilt backing*
- *1 piece of quilt batting, 30″ × 40″*
- *4 white shank-backed buttons (for noses), of ¾″ diameter*
- *8 white 4-holed buttons (for eyes) of ¾″ diameter*
- *White and yellow all-purpose sewing threads*
- *4 yards yellow ½″ extra-wide, double-fold bias binding (2″ wide when unfolded)*
- *White, pink, blue, yellow, and green embroidery floss.*

Directions

Overview: The wall hanging is made up of 4 bunny blocks in four pastel colors (see photo), on a white background, surrounded by a floral border. The pattern pieces used are the same for all 4 bunny blocks, but the colors of the materials are varied (see color photo). Instructions are given to make the first (blue) bunny block. Repeat these instructions with the appropriately colored materials for each of the 3 remaining blocks. Colors that change from block to block are given in brackets [ ]. R indicates that a pattern piece was reversed before cutting the fabric. E(R) is reversed piece E, for example. *Note:* All pattern pieces include ¼″ seam allowances. Piecing is done with right sides of fabric facing.

1. Trace patterns A through H for the bow-tie bunnies, and transfer the patterns to cardboard. Be sure to transfer all markings, including fold lines and seamlines. Trace and cut the pieces from the appropriate fabrics, as indicated in the pattern captions. Label the reversed pieces with an "R" to

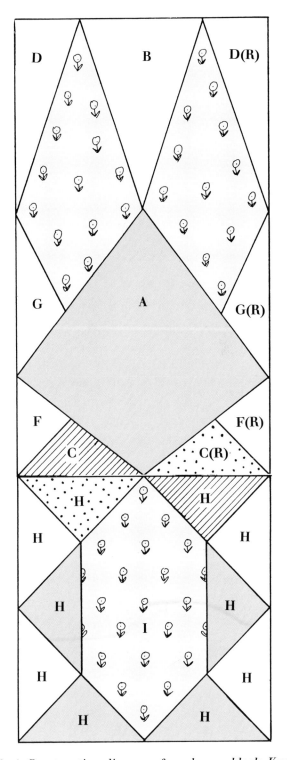

2–1 Construction diagram for a bunny block. Key:

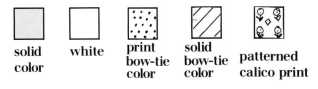

solid color   white   print bow-tie color   solid bow-tie color   patterned calico print

avoid confusion later. You may want to cut
the bunnies one at a time and piece each
one as you go along, to avoid having many
small pieces around. See photo for correct
colors of bow-tie triangles to cut for each
bunny.

2. Transfer markings for facial features onto
all "A" pieces.

3. Use white thread for piecing, and refer to
the construction diagram (Fig. 2–1) and
other diagrams to assemble a bunny block,
as detailed in steps 4–15 below. Press the
block after the addition of each piece.

Making a Bunny Block

4. For the left ear unit (Unit I), seam triangle
D on its long side to [blue] print piece E as
shown in Fig. 2–2.

5. Join triangle D(R) and [blue] print E(R) for
the right ear unit (Unit II); see Fig. 2–3.

6. Attach a white triangle G to Unit I as shown
in Figure 2–2. Attach white triangle G(R) to
the right ear unit (see Fig. 2–3).

7. Join white triangle B to the sides of units I
and II as shown in Figure 2–4.

8. Set in head piece A by stitching it to the unit
made in Step 7, as shown in Fig. 2–4. When
joining the units, seam them together
starting at the dots, leaving the seam
allowances free. When joining two units
that have an angle, insert the needle at the
angle and pivot the material before sewing
the second side (see General Directions
chapter for more details). Set the unit aside.

9. Take a white F triangle and a solid [yellow]
C triangle and join them as shown in Figure
2–5 to make Unit III (the left upper bow-tie
unit). Repeat this process with C(R) in
printed [yellow] fabric and a white F(R)
triangle to make the right upper bow-tie
unit (Unit IV); see Fig. 2–5.

10. Stitch Unit III to the lower left side of A (the
head) and stitch Unit IV to the lower right
side of A (see Fig. 2–6). This completes the
upper block section.

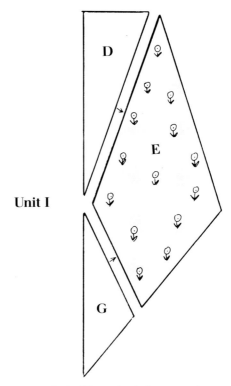

2–2 Piece the left ear unit
(Unit I).

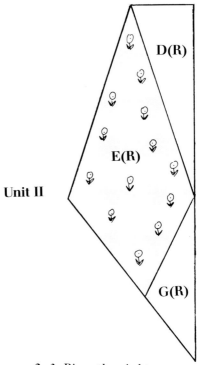

2–3 Piece the right ear
unit (Unit II), using
reverse-cut pieces.

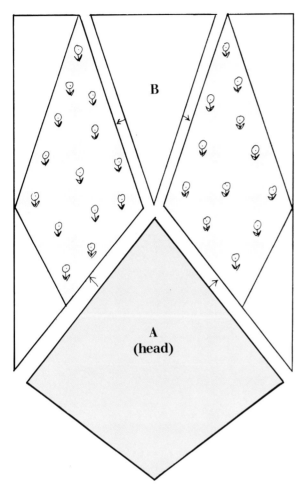

2–4 Set in triangle B between the ear units; set in piece A (the head) as shown.

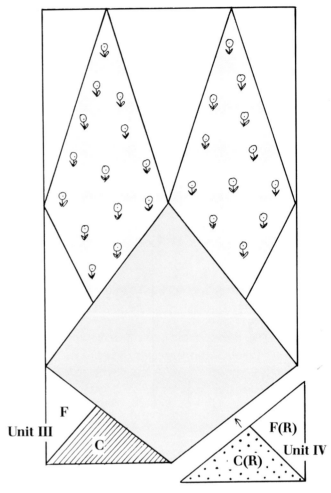

2–6 Join the upper bow-tie units to complete the upper block section.

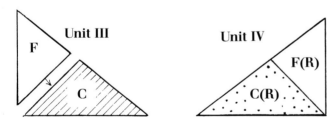

2–5 The upper bow-tie units, Unit III (left) and Unit IV (right).

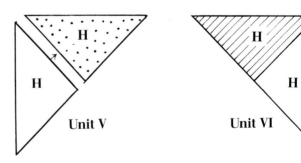

2–7 Piece the lower bow-tie units, Unit V (left) and Unit VI (right).

11. Take a white H triangle and a [yellow] print H triangle, and seam them together as shown in Figure 2–7 to make the lower left bow-tie unit (Unit V). Repeat this process using a second white H triangle and the [yellow] solid H triangle to make the lower

right bow-tie unit (Unit VI); see Fig. 2–7. Set them aside for now.

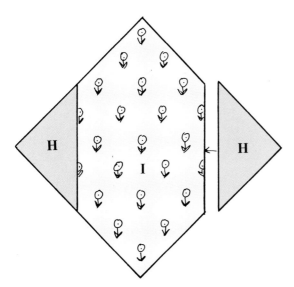

2–8 Seam two H triangles to the I piece.

12. Take the [blue] print piece I and two [blue] H triangles. Stitch the triangles to I as shown in Figure 2–8 to make the pieced square for the body unit.

13. Join a white H triangle and a solid [blue] H triangle as shown in Fig. 2–9 to make the left foot unit (Unit VII). Repeat for the right foot unit (Unit VIII). Join the foot units to the pieced square (Fig. 2–10).

14. Stitch Unit V (made in Step 11) to the top left edge of the body unit (the pieced square made in Step 12), as shown in Figure 2–10 (top). Stitch Unit VI to the top right edge of the pieced square (see Fig. 2–10). Stitch Unit VII and VIII to the pieced square at the bottom edges (see Fig. 2–10).This completes the lower block section.

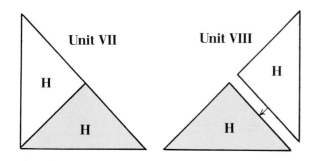

2–9 Piece the foot units, Unit VII (left) *and Unit VIII* (right).

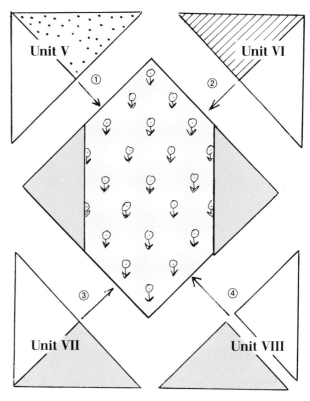

2–10 Attach the bow-tie units and foot units to the pieced square to make the lower block section.

15. Stitch the upper block section to the lower block section (Fig. 2–11). This completes the piecing of the bunny block.

16. Referring to the color photograph, complete the remaining 3 bunny blocks in the same way as you made the first one (steps 1 to 15).

Joining the Blocks and Finishing the Hanging

17. Stitch the 4 bunny blocks together along their long edges. Press the seams open.

18. Cut two side borders, 3½″ × 22½″ each, from the floral printed material, and stitch one to each short side of the 4-block bunny unit.

19. Cut a top and bottom border, each 3½″ × 38½″; stitch them to the top and bottom of the unit made in Step 18. Press the seams toward the outside edges.

20. Embroider whiskers, using 2 strands of white floss, in the stem stitch (see "Hand Embroidery" in the General Directions chapter). Embroider the mouth in the stem stitch using 2 strands of floss that matches the color of each bunny's bow tie (e.g., a yellow mouth on the blue bunny).

21. Cut the wall hanging backing to size 30″ × 40″. Lay the backing face-down on your work surface. Center the batting over the backing. Center the quilt top, face-up, over the batting. Pin and baste the layers together.

22. Machine-quilt the wall hanging, referring to the General Directions chapter for machine-quilting information.

23. Bind the wall hanging with yellow binding (see General Directions for binding information).

24. Stitch noses (shank buttons) to the bunnies where indicated by X in circles on A, using a doubled length of white thread. Attach the eyes (4-holed buttons) as indicated on A, using 2 strands of floss in colors matching the bunnies' mouths. Stitch whiskers and upper lips (dotted lines on A) in a contrasting color of embroidery thread, using 3 strands of embroidery floss.

25. Make a sleeve from which to hang the wall hanging and attach it (see General Directions).

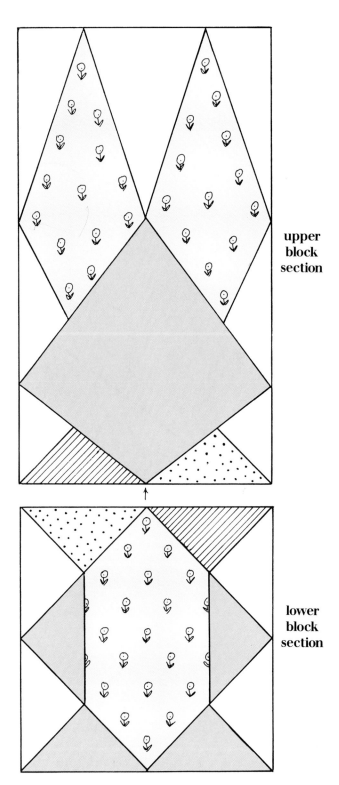

upper block section

lower block section

2–11 Stitch the upper and lower block sections together to complete one bunny block.

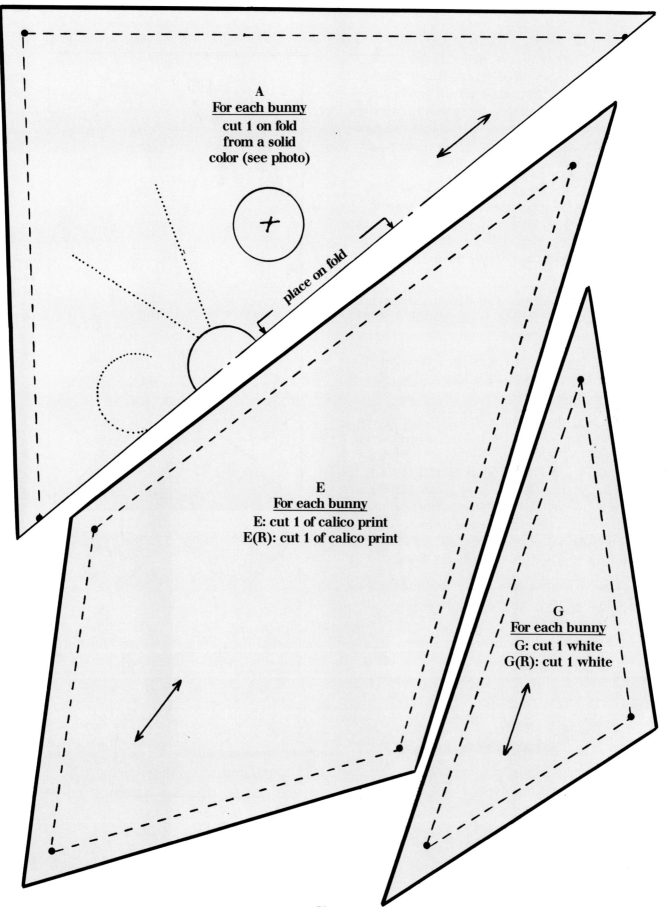

A
For each bunny
cut 1 on fold
from a solid
color (see photo)

place on fold

E
For each bunny
E: cut 1 of calico print
E(R): cut 1 of calico print

G
For each bunny
G: cut 1 white
G(R): cut 1 white

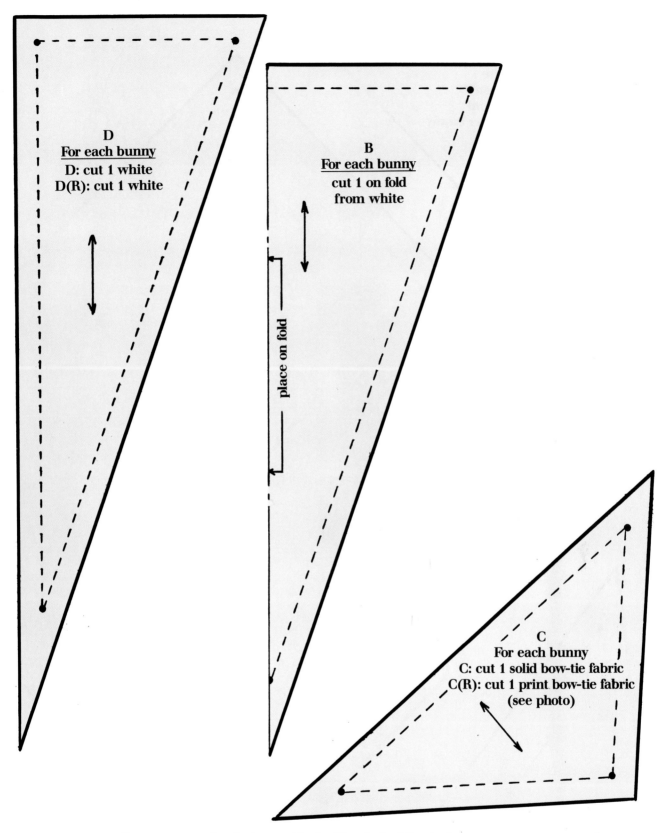

D
For each bunny
D: cut 1 white
D(R): cut 1 white

B
For each bunny
**cut 1 on fold
from white**

place on fold

C
For each bunny
C: cut 1 solid bow-tie fabric
C(R): cut 1 print bow-tie fabric
(see photo)

Pages 30–32. *Full-size patterns for the bunny blocks. The dashed line is the seamline. The solid line is the cutting line.*

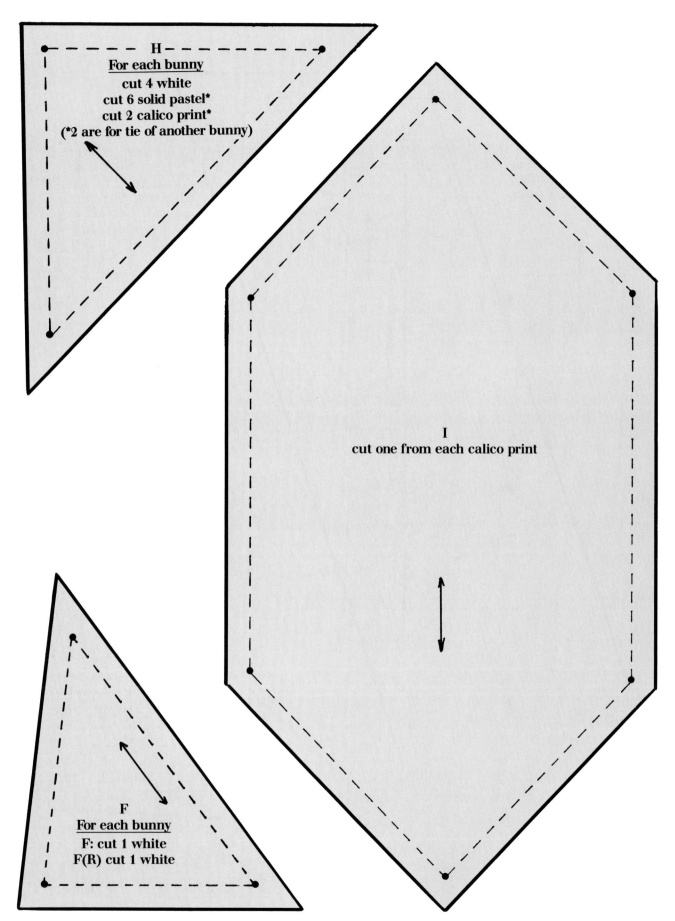

H
For each bunny
cut 4 white
cut 6 solid pastel*
cut 2 calico print*
(*2 are for tie of another bunny)

I
cut one from each calico print

F
For each bunny
F: cut 1 white
F(R) cut 1 white

Floral Runner and Sachet

The sachet and dresser runner add a dainty accent to your bedroom; the colors can be modified to match any decor. Finished size of runner: 14″ × 34″, excluding lace. Finished size of sachet: approximately 5″ × 7″.

Materials Required for Set

- *1 yard ecru broadcloth*
- *¼ yard each rose and green solid fabrics*
- *Sewing threads to match fabrics*
- *3 yards 1"-wide gathered ecru lace*
- *½ yard fusible transfer webbing*
- *⅓ yard of ¼"-wide green satin ribbon*
- *1 cup potpourri (optional)*

Directions

Note: All measurements, except appliqué patterns, include ¼" seam allowances.

Runner

1. Cut two 14¼" × 34½" rectangles from the ecru fabric. Fold one rectangle into quarters and press it. Set aside the second rectangle to be used as the backing. Trace and cut out the corner cutting guide pattern (Fig. 3–1) from paper. Position the cutting guide under your prepressed ecru rectangle, aligning centerlines and edges, and trace around the cutting guide at *each* corner with light blue washable pencil, but *do not cut the fabric yet.* This will be the runner top.

2. Trace 2 sets of the reversed flowers, circles, and leaves from the appliqué pattern (Fig. 3–2) onto fusible webbing. Cut out the flowers and large circles from the webbing and fuse them onto the back of the rose fabric. Cut them out of the fabric plus webbing.

3. Cut out the leaves and small circles from the webbing and fuse them onto the back of the green fabric. Cut them out of the fabric plus webbing.

4. On the flowers made in Step 2, cut out and discard the areas that are indicated by cross-hatching on Figure 3–2.

5. With washable light blue pencil, lightly trace the entire appliqué pattern (Fig. 3–2) at each end of the ecru runner top, including the cross-hatching lines. Face the flowers in opposite directions (see photo). Position the appliqué pattern so that the right edge of the flower is 3" from the runner's edge at the center of the short side.

6. Following the traced appliqué pattern, fuse the flowers, circles, and leaves in position on the runner top.

7. Machine-appliqué the flowers and leaves in place on the runner top with matching threads, using a medium-width (⅛" wide) machine satin stitch.

8. Machine satin-stitch with green thread along the stem and leaf lines. Narrow the width of the satin-stitch setting on the machine to the narrowest stitch possible; then satin-stitch along the cross-hatching of the flowers.

9. Cut the corners of the runner top along the lines you marked with the corner cutting guide in Step 1 (see Fig. 3–3).

10. Trace the corner cutting guide onto the ecru backing piece as well, and cut out the corners on it also. Set it aside.

11. With the gathered edge of the lace aligned with the raw edge of the appliquéd runner top, baste the lace to the right side of the appliquéd runner top (Fig. 3–4).

12. With right sides of material facing each other, stitch the runner top and backing together all around with a ¼" seam allowance, leaving a 4" opening along one long edge for turning. Clip the seam allowances at the corners for easier turning, turn the runner right-side out, and press it. Stitch the opening closed by hand.

13. Machine-stitch very close to the edge all around the runner, to keep the layers from shifting.

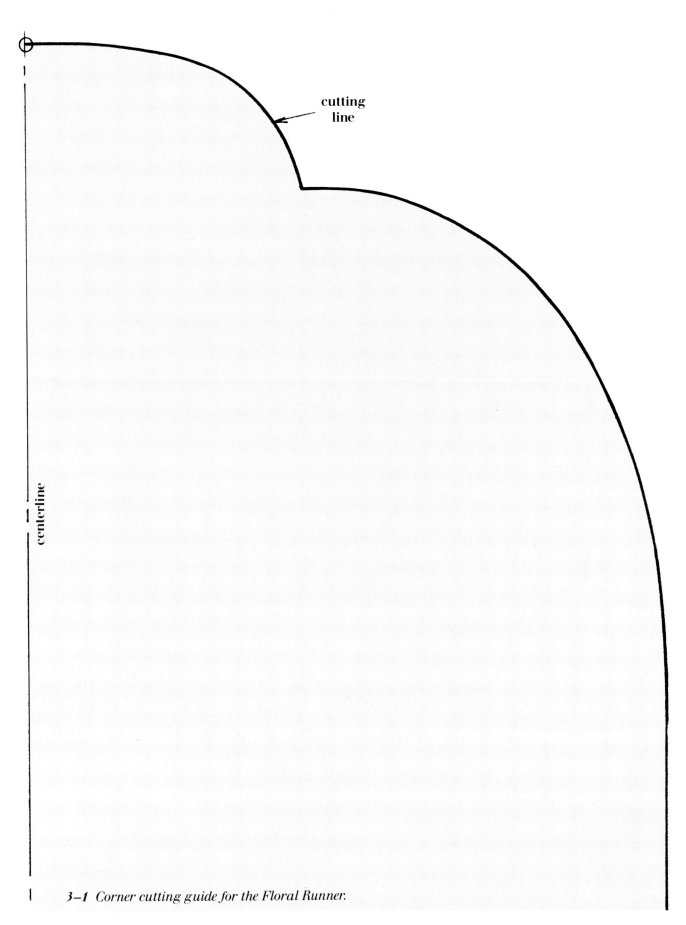

cutting
line

centerline

3–1 *Corner cutting guide for the Floral Runner.*

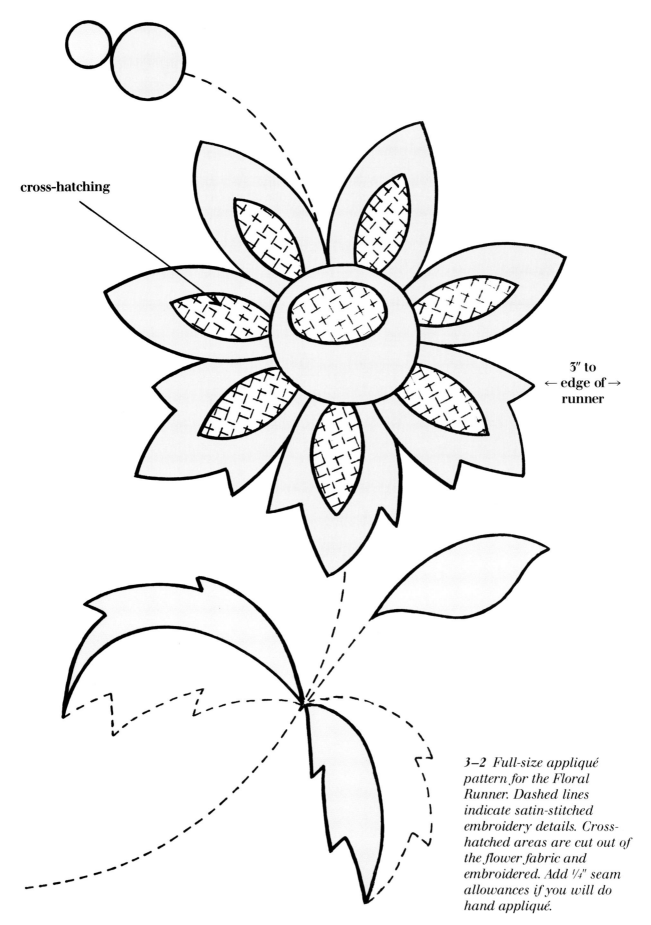

cross-hatching

3" to
← edge of →
runner

3–2 Full-size appliqué pattern for the Floral Runner. Dashed lines indicate satin-stitched embroidery details. Cross-hatched areas are cut out of the flower fabric and embroidered. Add ¼" seam allowances if you will do hand appliqué.

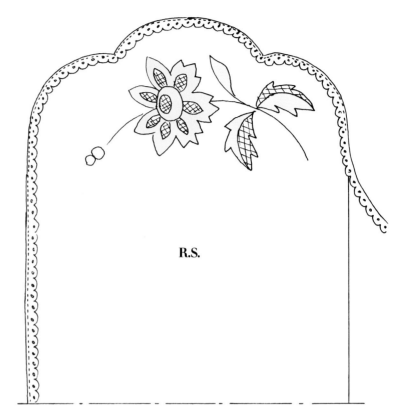

3–3 Diagram of the runner corner (¼ of runner is shown, reduced). Shaded area is cut away.

3–4 Applying the lace edging (½ of runner is shown, reduced). Align the gathered edge of the lace with the raw edge of the runner top on the right side of the runner top. Continue applying lace with a ¼" seam allowance until the runner top is completely edged with lace.

Sachet

1. Cut 2 rectangles from the ecru fabric, using the full-size sachet pattern (Fig. 3–5), and lightly trace the appliqué design with washable blue pencil onto the right side of one rectangle of fabric, which will be the front of the sachet.

2. Trace one reversed flower and leaf from Figure 3–5 onto fusible webbing.

3. Cut out and fuse the webbing flower to the back of the rose fabric. Cut out the flower from the rose fabric plus webbing. Cut out the cross-hatched area from the flower and discard it. Fuse the flower in position on the marked sachet front you made in Step 1.

4. Cut out the webbing leaf and fuse it to the back of the green fabric. Cut out the leaf from the green fabric, and fuse it in position on the sachet front.

5. Machine-appliqué the flower and leaf to the sachet front, and machine-embroider the stem, flower, and leaf details; see runner instructions (steps 7 and 8) for details.

6. Stitch the sachet front and back together, with right sides facing, along the sides and bottom. Clip the bottom corners off the seam allowance (without clipping the seam) to ease turning, turn the bag right-side out, and press it.

7. Zigzag stitch around the top edge of the bag to keep it from ravelling. Turn ¼" of the top edge inside the bag and stitch it down to secure it. Attach lace around the top of the bag, with its gathered edge on the inside of the bag. Fill the bag with potpourri and tie it with ribbon.

cutting line   stitching line

3–5 Full-size sachet pattern and appliqué. Solid outer line is cutting line. Dashed outer line is seamline.

Rosebuds Tea Cozy, Tablecloth, and Napkins

Wouldn't your favorite tea drinker just love this elegant set? Hand appliqué makes it extra special! Finished size of tablecloth: 32" × 32". Finished size of tea cozy: 12" × 12", excluding ruffle. Finished size of napkin: 16" × 16".

Materials Required for Set

- *2 yards white broadcloth*
- *1 yard light pink (LP) broadcloth*
- *½ yard dark pink (DP) broadcloth*
- *¼ yard each of medium green (MG), light yellow (LY), and medium yellow (MY) broadcloth*
- *2 squares of polyester craft fleece (or stiff, low-loft batting), 12½" × 12½" each*
- *Light pink, dark pink, medium green, and medium yellow embroidery floss*
- *Sewing threads to match fabrics*
- *1 yard yellow ¼" extra-wide double-fold bias binding (opened width = 2")*
- *1 yard yellow piping*
- *6" piece of ½"-wide white ribbon*

Directions

Note: Measurements include ¼" seam allowances, except for the appliqué patterns. The instructions are written for hand appliqué. See the section on machine appliqué in the General Directions chapter if you want to make the project using machine appliqué.

Tea Cozy

1. Enlarge the Tea Cozy pattern (Fig. 4–1). (See enlarging tips in the General Directions chapter.)

2. Cut two 12½" squares from white broadcloth and two from light pink broadcloth. Set the pink squares aside for the lining. Set aside one white piece for the cozy backing, pattern (4–1), but don't cut it out yet.

3. Trace out the tea cozy appliqué pattern (Fig. 4–2) onto a piece of tracing paper. Flip the pattern over, align the centerline, and trace the left two roses and bow, and stem details, onto a second piece of tracing paper to complete the pattern (see photo). Join the two pieces together to make the whole appliqué pattern.

4. Take one 12½" square of white material cut in Step 2, fold it in half, and press it. It will become the front of the tea cozy. Trace out the tea cozy pattern, enlarged from Fig. 4–1, onto the square, but don't cut it out yet. Next, center the tea cozy front over the completed appliqué pattern and trace the appliqué pattern onto the right side of the fabric (see the photograph for reference), using washable light blue pencil. Use the washable light blue pencil for all further tracing on fabric.

5. Trace 3 dark pink and 2 light pink roses onto the right sides of their respective fabrics from the appliqué pattern (Fig. 4–2); trace the rose embroidery markings as well. Add ¼" seam allowances around each rose and cut them out of their respective fabrics. *Note:* for steps 5 through 8, do not add seam allowances if you are doing machine appliqué.

6. Fold under the seam allowances of the appliqué pieces to the wrong side of each rose; baste the seam allowances in place if you wish, and appliqué the roses in place by hand onto the tea cozy front.

7. Trace the leaves from Figure 4–2 onto the green fabric, add ¼" seam allowance around each, and cut them out. Hand appliqué the leaves onto the tea cozy front, using green thread.

8. For the bow, trace the tails and bow body onto medium yellow material, add ¼" seam allowance around them, and cut them out. Trace the loop ovals in the bow onto light yellow material, add ¼" seam allowance, and cut out. Appliqué the bows to the tea cozy front with matching thread.

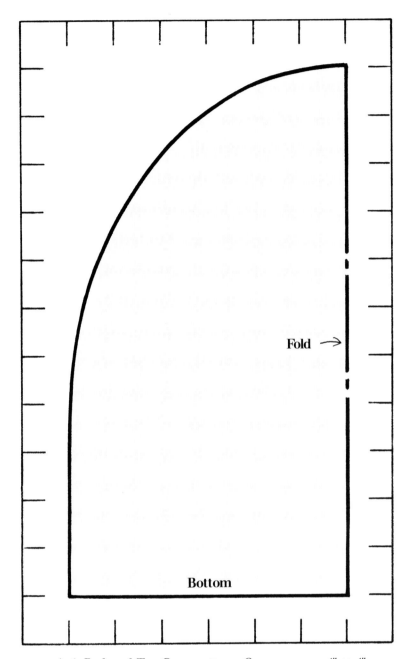

Fold →

Bottom

*4–1 Reduced Tea Cozy pattern. One square = 1″ × 1″.
Enlarge and cut 1 on folded paper.*

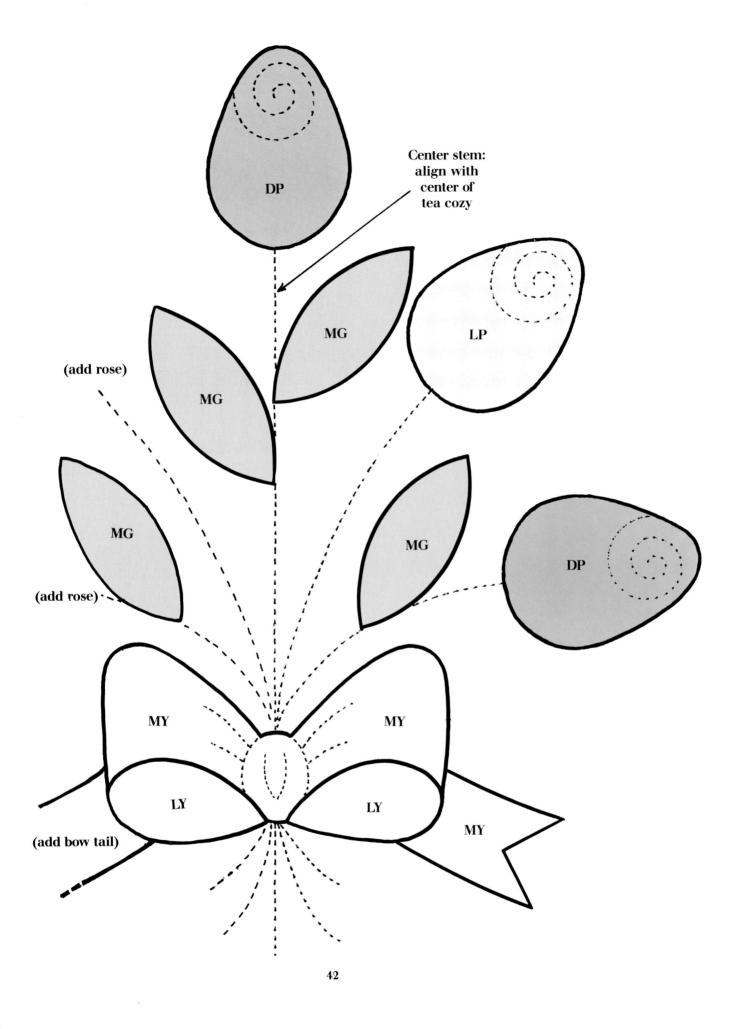

DP

Center stem:
align with
center of
tea cozy

MG

LP

(add rose)

MG

MG

MG

DP

(add rose)

MY

MY

LY

LY

MY

(add bow tail)

42

9. Embroider the stems by hand in stem stitch (see pg. 13), using three strands of green floss. Embroider the rosebuds' center swirls with 3 strands of light pink floss on the dark pink roses and with dark pink floss on the light pink roses. Press. Embroider the bow details in yellow floss.

10. Baste a 12½″ square of fleece to the wrong side of the appliquéd square about ¼″ in from the outline of the cozy. Trace the enlarged cozy pattern onto the white square you reserved for the cozy back in Step 2, and baste the second square of fleece to it in the same way. Cut out the front of the cozy, with its attached fleece. Use the cozy front as a pattern to cut out the cozy back, and from the pink squares you cut in Step 2, cut out two of enlarged cozy pattern for the lining.

11. Fold the piece of white ribbon in half to make a loop. Baste the loop to the right side of the center top of the appliquéd cozy front so that the ends of the ribbon extend ¼″ beyond the cozy front's top raw edge and the loop is facing in (see Fig. 4–3). Baste yellow piping around the curved edges on the outside of the cozy front, so that the raw edge of the piping is even with the raw edge of the cozy front. Do not place piping along the bottom edge. (See the General Directions chapter for more information on piping.)

12. For the ruffle, cut one 4″ × 30″ strip from the light pink material. Fold the strip in half lengthwise, with right sides together. Stitch it along the short sides. Turn it right-side out and press it. Baste through the raw edges of the long sides of the folded strip; gather the long raw edges to make the ruffle. Baste the ruffle to the curved outside edge of the tea cozy front (Fig. 4–4), evenly distributing the fullness; the raw edge of the ruffle should align with the raw edge of the cozy front and piping.

4–3 Baste the ribbon loop to the right side of the cozy front.

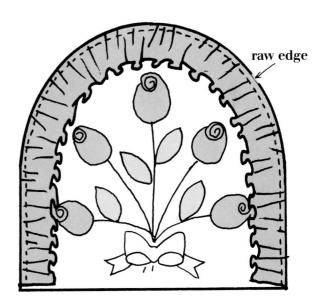

raw edge

4–4 Baste the raw edges of the ruffle along the raw curved edge of the front of the cozy, on the right side of the fabric.

4–2 Opposite page: Partial appliqué pattern for Rosebuds Tea Set, full size. Add missing roses and bow tail to left-hand side by tracing out patterns for the rose and bow tail and reversing them (see photo). Embroider the stems in green. Embroider bow details in yellow. Embroider the swirls in the roses in pink.

13. With right sides of the fabric together, baste and stitch the tea cozy front to the tea cozy back along the curved edge, leaving the bottom (straight edge) open. Turn it right-side out and set it aside.

14. Take the two pink pieces for the cozy lining you cut in Step 10. With right sides facing, stitch them together along the curved edge, leaving the bottom edge open.

15. Insert the lining into the tea cozy with the wrong sides of the lining and tea cozy facing each other. Align the side seams and baste the lining to the cozy around the bottom edges. Bind the bottom edge with the yellow bias binding (see the General Directions chapter for binding instructions). Press.

Tablecloth

1. Cut one 32½″ square of white fabric for the backing and set it aside. Cut one 28½″ square of white fabric, fold it into quarters on the diagonals, and press it to mark placement lines for the appliqués. Unfold the square; it will become the top layer of the tablecloth.

2. Align a corner of the 28½″ square over the full-sized appliqué pattern and trace the stem lines for the upper 3 roses of the pattern (see the photo for reference). Use washable light blue pencil for tracing of all appliqués. The ends of the stems should be approximately 3″ from the corner of the fabric. Trace the appliqué in the remaining three corners of the tablecloth top in the same way. Cut out and appliqué 3 roses and 2 leaves to each corner (see photograph), as you did for the tea cozy. Appliqué one yellow bow to each corner, as you did for the tea cozy. Embroider the stem lines, rose swirls, and bow details (see steps 5 through 9 of the Tea Cozy instructions).

3. For the borders, cut two strips, each 2½″ × 28½″, from light pink material. With right sides of fabric facing, stitch them to two opposite sides of the appliquéd square, with a seam allowance of ¼″.

4. To complete the border, cut two strips of light pink material, each 2½″ × 32½″, and stitch them with ¼″ seam allowance and right sides of fabric facing to the unbordered sides of the unit you made in Step 3. Press the tablecloth top.

5. Stitch the tablecloth top to the backing you cut in Step 1, with right sides of material together and ¼″ seam allowances, leaving a 4″ opening along one side through which to turn the cloth. Trim off the seam allowances a bit and clip the corners of the seam allowances to facilitate turning. Turn the unit right-side out. Hand-stitch the 4″ opening closed and press the tablecloth. Stitch around the tablecloth along the line where the white appliquéd square meets the pink border, in order to keep the layers from shifting.

Napkins

1. For each napkin, cut one 17″ square from white fabric.

2. Turn under each raw edge ¼″ and ¼″ again, and stitch it down to make a double hem.

3. Trace a flower and two leaves from Fig. 4–2 onto the napkin top with light blue washable pencil. The end of the stems should be about 1″ from the corner (see photo).

4. Appliqué one flower and two leaves to one corner of each napkin, and embroider the details (see the Tea Cozy instructions, steps 5 through 9, for appliqué and embroidery information).

Spring Baby Quilt and Bib

Surprise a new mother with this set. Remember to include washing instructions: Machine wash with cold water; dry on the "delicate" setting. Quilt size: Approximately 36″ × 36″. Bib size: 11″ × 13″.

Materials Required for Set

- *1 yard white broadcloth*

- *½ yard each dark green broadcloth and rose broadcloth*

- *1 yard each rose print and teal print fabrics*

- *38″ × 38″ piece of fabric for quilt backing*

- *38″ × 38″ piece of quilt batting*

- *12″ × 15″ piece of fabric for bib backing*

- *12″ × 15″ piece of fleece for bib*

- *1 yard fusible transfer webbing*

- *Sewing threads to match fabrics*

- *7 yards white ½″ extra-wide double-fold binding (unfolded width, 2″)*

Directions

Note: ¼″ seam allowances are included in all given measurements, except for appliqué patterns.

Quilt

1. Cut one 24½″ square from white broadcloth. Fold the square into quarters and press it to mark the center.

2. Trace 12 large flowers and 12 large stems onto fusible webbing from Fig. 5–2, and cut them out of the webbing.

3. Fuse 6 of the webbing flowers to the back of the solid rose broadcloth and 6 to the rose print fabric, and cut them out.

4. Fuse the webbing stems to the back of the green broadcloth, and cut them out. Arrange the stems with 3 stems in each quarter of the white square you cut in Step 1 (see Fig. 5–1); the bottom points of the stems should be 2″ from the center of the square. Fuse the print and solid-colored tulips alternately above the stems (see Fig. 5–1 and the photo).

5. Appliqué the flower and stem pieces in place with matching threads, using a mid-width machine satin stitch. Press the appliquéd square.

6. Cut 2 strips of rose print fabric, each 2½″ × 24½″. Stitch the strips to 2 opposite sides of the appliquéd square.

7. Cut 2 strips of rose print fabric 2½″ × 28½″, and stitch them to the top and bottom of the unit you made in Step 6.

8. Cut 2 strips of teal print fabric, each 4½″ × 28½″, and stitch them to the left and right sides of the unit made in Step 7.

9. Cut two teal strips, each 4½″ × 36½″, and stitch them to the top and bottom of the unit made in Step 8. Press.

10. Lay the quilt backing piece face-down on your work surface. Center the quilt batting over the backing; center the quilt top face-up over the batting. Pin-baste or baste the three layers together.

5–1 Appliqué placement diagram. Fuse three flowers and three stems to each quarter of the quilt.

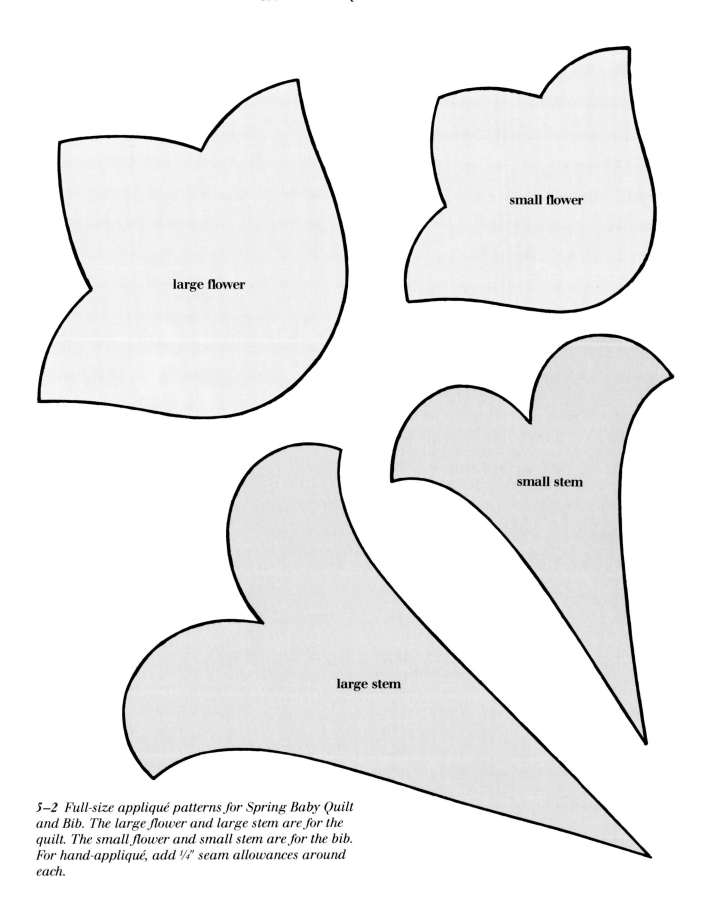

5–2 Full-size appliqué patterns for Spring Baby Quilt and Bib. The large flower and large stem are for the quilt. The small flower and small stem are for the bib. For hand-appliqué, add ¼" seam allowances around each.

11. Quilt along all the seamlines; quilt again ¼″ in from the seamlines. Also quilt close to the outside edges of the appliqué pieces. Quilt another line of stitching ¼″ outside the line around the appliqué pieces. Then quilt another line ¼″ outside of the last one you did.

12. Baste through all 3 layers, ¼″ inside the raw edges of the quilt top. Trim away the excess batting and backing. Bind the quilt top with the white binding (see the General Directions for binding details).

Bib

1. Cut a 5″ × 10½″ rectangle from white broadcloth. Fold it in half lengthwise and press it to mark the centerline.

2. Trace the small stem and small flower from Figure 5–1 onto the fusible webbing, and cut each out.

3. Fuse the webbing stem to the back of the green broadcloth, and fuse the webbing flower to the back of the rose print fabric and cut them out. Fuse the stem in place on the white rectangle, so its pointed end is ¾″ from the bottom edge of the rectangle and it is centered on the centerline. Fuse the flower above the stem (see photo).

4. Cut two 1½″ × 10½″ strips from rose broadcloth, and stitch them to the two long sides of the white rectangle. Press the unit. Cut one 1½″ × 7½″ strip of rose broadcloth and stitch it to the bottom of the rectangle.

5. Cut two 2½ × 10½″ strips from the teal print fabric, and stitch them to the sides of the unit made in Step 4. Cut one 2½″ × 11½″ strip from the teal print and stitch it to the bottom of the unit. Press. This completes the bib top.

6. Place the bib backing (12″ × 15″ fabric) face-down on your work surface. Center the fleece over the backing; center the bib top over the fleece. Pin-baste the layers together, and quilt them as you did for the quilt (steps 11–12). Baste around the edges of the bib front, through all 3 layers, and trim away the excess backing and fleece.

7. Center Figure 5–4 on the bib's center, trace the cutting line lightly onto the material, and cut out the curve in the neck area (see Fig. 5–3). Baste the layers together close to the cut edge.

8. Bind the bib's sides and the bottom with the white binding. Keeping the remaining white binding in one piece, make the ties and bind the neck edge at the same time, as follows: Find the center of the binding strip, and pin one raw edge to the center of the neck curve. Continue pinning on both sides of the center until you reach the ends of the bib. Baste the binding in place; remove the pins (Fig. 5–5). Fold the binding up and around to the back of the bib. Starting at one tail end of the binding, stitch the binding closed at the edges; continue the stitching along the neck curve, enclosing the raw edges of the neck edge in the binding. Continue stitching to the opposite tail end of the binding strip. Tuck the raw edges of each binding end into itself and stitch it down to secure it.

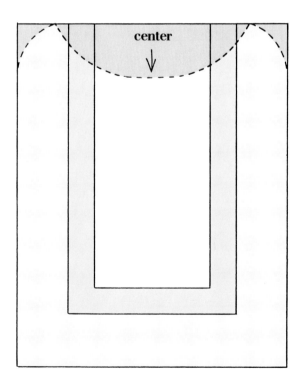

5–3 Neck edge cutting diagram (reduced). The dashed line is the cutting line. Shaded area is cut away.

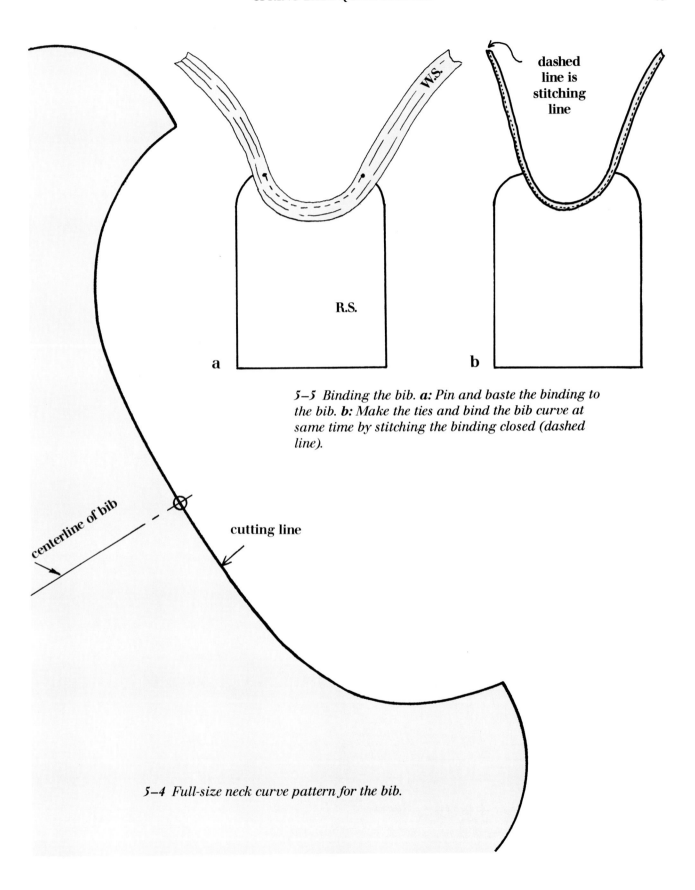

R.S.

W.S.

dashed
line is
stitching
line

a   b

*5–5 Binding the bib. **a:** Pin and baste the binding to the bib. **b:** Make the ties and bind the bib curve at same time by stitching the binding closed (dashed line).*

centerline of bib

cutting line

5–4 Full-size neck curve pattern for the bib.

Celebrating Summer

June Bride Pillow

This project will be especially pretty when matched to the wedding colors. Finished size of pillow: 12½″ × 12½″.

Materials Required

- *½ yard each white fabric and pink fabric*
- *White and pink sewing threads*
- *Medium pink and light green embroidery floss*
- *2 yards of pink piping*
- *4 pink ribbon roses*
- *2 yards of ¼"-wide white satin ribbon*
- *⅓ yard fusible transfer webbing*
- *12" × 12" pillow form*

Directions

Note: ¼" seam allowances are included in all measurements, except for the appliqué patterns.

1. Trace a full 9"-diameter circle onto fusible webbing; ¼ of the circle pattern is given in Figure 6–1. Cut out and fuse the webbing circle to the back of the pink fabric. Cut the circle out of the pink fabric and set it aside.

2. Trace one reversed dove (Fig. 6–2) onto the back of fusible webbing, cut it out, and fuse it to the back of the white fabric. Transfer all markings to the fabric dove and cut it out of the fabric.

3. Cut two 12½" squares from white fabric. Set aside one square for the backing. Fuse the pink circle cut in Step 1 to the front of the remaining white fabric square so the circle is centered on the square's center. Fuse the dove cut in Step 2 to the front of the pink circle (see photo). Transfer the embroidery markings to the beak area of the circle.

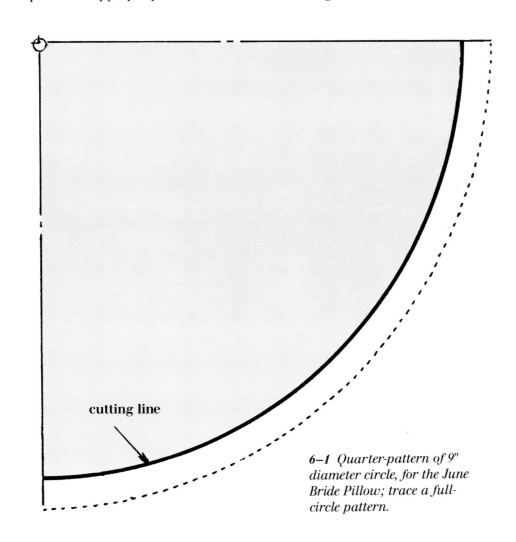

cutting line

6–1 Quarter-pattern of 9" diameter circle, for the June Bride Pillow; trace a full-circle pattern.

4. Machine-appliqué the circle and the dove onto the square with threads that match the fabrics, using a medium-width satin stitch. Machine satin-stitch along the dashed lines on the dove that indicate the wing (see Fig. 6–2).

5. Using 3 strands of pink embroidery floss, embroider the flower buds by hand as French knots (see the General Directions for hand embroidery stitches). In stem stitch, embroider the stems by hand, using 2 strands of green embroidery floss. Embroider a circle of featherstitch, using 2 strands of green floss, ¼" outside the edge of the circle, in the white area. If your machine can mock a handmade featherstitch, feel free to let your machine do the work! Embroider 5 French knot buds, one in each position indicated by an "X" on Figure 6–3. Embroider a green eye on the bird, with a French knot.

6. Cut two 20" lengths of ribbon. Tie each one into a 2"-wide bow with equal tails. Tack the bows at the beak area (see photo). Cut the remaining ribbon into 4 equal lengths and tie each length into a 2"-wide bow. Stitch the bow to the white fabric at the positions indicated by black dots on Figure 6–3. Tack

6–2 Appliqué and embroidery pattern for the June Bride Pillow. The dashed lines of wing markings are satin-stitched (see text).

one pink ribbon rose near each bow (see photo).

7. On the right side of the pillow top, baste piping around the edges, with raw edges of the piping and the pillow top aligned. Place the pillow top on the pillow backing with right sides of material together and stitch along 3 sides; leave the bottom edge open.

8. Clip the corners of the seam allowances, and turn the pillow cover right-side out. Insert the pillow form, and stitch the opening closed.

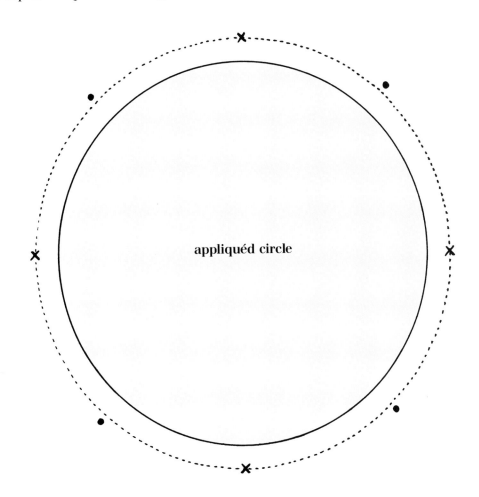

appliquéd circle

6–3 Diagram of the appliquéd circle (reduced). "x" indicates a French knot; a black dot indicates bow placement.

July 4th Picnic Quilt and Apron

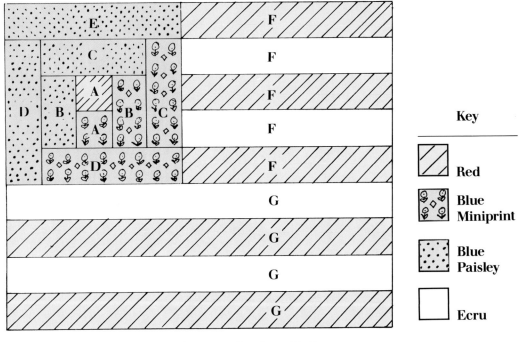

7–1 Construction diagram for the quilt flag block.

Muted colors give this set old-fashioned appeal. Finished size of quilt: 62″ × 78″ (finished block size: 22″ × 18″). Apron size: 26″ × 34″.

Materials Required for Set

- *2 yards ecru fabric*
- *1 yard blue miniprint fabric*
- *3 yards blue paisley print*
- *2 yards red miniprint fabric*
- *68″ × 84″ piece of fabric for quilt backing*
- *68″ × 84″ piece of traditional-weight quilt batting*
- *28″ × 35″ piece of fabric for apron backing*
- *4 yards navy blue ½″ extra-wide double-fold bias binding (unfolded width = 2″)*
- *6 yards ecru ½″-wide bias binding (unfolded width = 2″)*

7–2 Construction diagram for the pieced blue square for the quilt and the apron. Unfinished size, 10½″ × 10½″, including seam allowance.

Directions

Quilt

Overview: The quilt is made up of six flag blocks (Fig. 7–1). Each block has a pieced blue square with a red center (Fig. 7–2) in a log-cabin style pattern, and red stripes. All measurements include ¼″ seam allowances. Piecing is done with right sides of fabric facing.

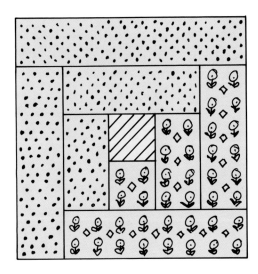

Cutting Guide for Quilt

From red miniprint fabric cut:

- *6 A squares, each 2½" × 2½"*
- *18 F strips, each 2½" × 12½"*
- *12 G strips, each 2½" × 22½"*

From blue miniprint fabric cut:

- *6 A squares, each 2½" × 2½"*
- *6 B strips, each 2½" × 4½"*
- *6 C strips, each 2½" × 6½"*
- *6 D strips, each 2½" × 8½"*

From blue paisley fabric cut:

- *6 B strips, each 2½" × 4½"*
- *6 C strips, each 2½" × 6½"*
- *6 D strips, each 2½" × 8½"*
- *6 E strips, each 2½" × 10½"*
- *4 J borders, each 6½" × 62½"*

(You may want to wait until your quilt center is pieced before you cut the borders, in case your central unit is slightly smaller or larger, but be sure to leave enough material for them)

From ecru fabric cut:

- *12 F strips, each 2½" × 12½"*
- *12 G strips, each 2½" × 22½"*
- *9 H sashing strips, each 2½" × 18½"*
- *4 I sashing strips, each 2½" × 50½"*

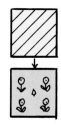

7–3 Join two A squares for the pieced blue square.

Piecing the Blue Squares

1. Join a red A square to a blue miniprint A square (Fig. 7–3).

2. Join a paisley B strip to the left side of the unit made in Step 1. Join a blue miniprint B strip to the right side of the unit (Fig. 7–4).

3. Join a paisley C strip along the top of the unit made in Step 2 (Fig. 7–5).

4. Join a blue miniprint C strip to the right side of the unit made in Step 3 (Fig. 7–6).

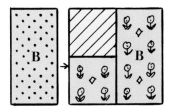

7–4 Join a paisley B strip to the left side and a blue miniprint B strip to the right side.

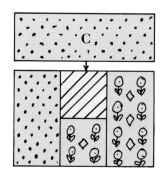

7–5 Join a paisley C strip to the top.

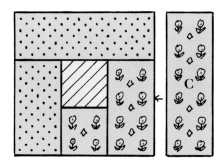

7–6 Join a blue miniprint C strip to the right.

5. Join a blue miniprint D strip to the bottom of the unit made in Step 4 (Fig. 7–7).

6. Join a blue paisley D strip to the left side of the unit made in Step 5 (Fig. 7–8).

7. Finish the square by adding a blue paisley E strip across the top (Fig. 7–9).

8. Make 5 more pieces blue squares like the one you made in steps 1–7.

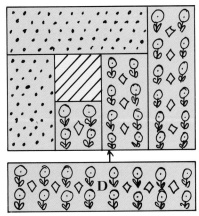

7–7 Join a blue miniprint D strip to the bottom.

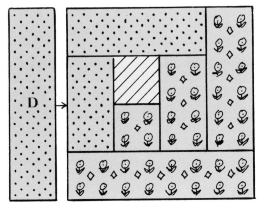

7–8 Join a paisley D strip to the left side.

Completing the Flag Blocks

9. Stitch three red F strips alternately with 2 ecru F strips along their long sides to make the 5-strip unit shown in Fig. 7–10b, pressing after each addition.

10. Make five more 5-strip units like the one you made in Step 9.

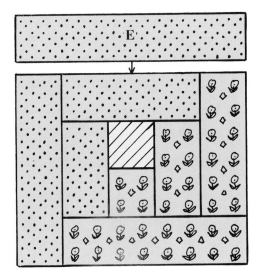

7–9 Join a paisley E strip to finish the pieced square.

11. Stitch each 5-strip unit to one of the blue log-cabin blocks, as shown in Figure 7–10b.

12. To make the lower flag unit, shown in Figure 7–10c, take 2 ecru G strips and 2 red G strips; alternate ecru G strips with red G strips as shown and seam them together on their long sides. Press.

13. Make five more lower flag units like the one pieced in Step 12.

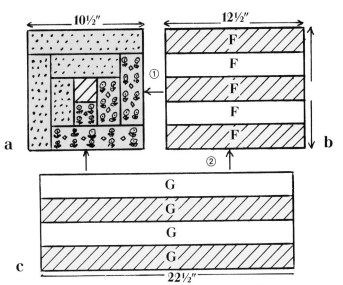

7–10 The three units of a flag block. a: The pieced square; b: The 5-strip unit; c: The lower flag unit.

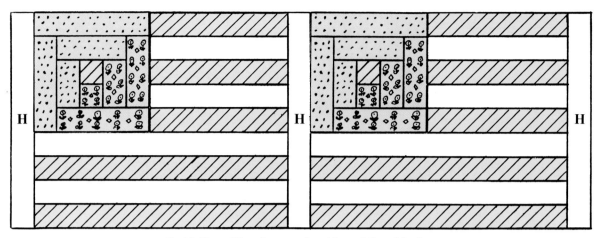

7–11 Ecru H strips on the sides of flag blocks.

14. Join the lower flag unit to the unit made in Step 11, as shown in Figure 7–10. The finished block is shown in Figure 7–1.

15. Repeat Step 14 to complete the other 5 flag blocks.

Joining the Blocks, Borders, and Finishing the Quilt

16. Join an ecru H sashing strip (2½″ × 18½″) to the left side of each flag block. Join an ecru H strip to the right side of three of the flag blocks as well.

17. Make three rows of two flags each, as shown in Figure 7–11, by joining the units made in Step 16.

18. Attach ecru I sashing strips, as shown in Figure 7–12, above, below, and between the rows made in Step 17. This completes the central part of the quilt.

19. Attach two paisley blue J borders to the sides of the central unit made in Step 18.

20. Attach two more J borders to the top and bottom of the unit made in Step 19. This completes the quilt top.

21. Take the quilt backing and lay it face-down on a clean floor. With masking tape, secure it to the floor with small pieces of tape,

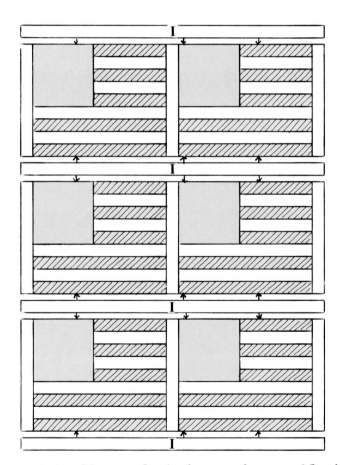

7–12 Attaching ecru I strips between the rows of flag blocks.

smoothing the wrinkles. Center the batting over the backing and center the quilt top over the batting. Pin-baste or hand-baste the layers together.

22. Using hand- or machine-quilting, quilt the picnic quilt in patterns that are pleasing to you. (The model is machine-quilted along all of the seamlines.)

23. Baste all three layers together close to the raw edges of the quilt top. Trim away the excess batting and backing. Bind the quilt with the ecru binding.

Cutting Guide for Apron

From red miniprint fabric cut:

- *1 A square, 2½″ × 2½″*
- *3 K strips, each 2½″ × 24½″*
- *4 L strips, each 2½″ × 34½″*

From blue miniprint fabric cut:

- *1 A square, 2½″ × 2½″*
- *1 B strip, 2½″ × 4½″*
- *1 C strip, 2½″ × 6½″*
- *1 D strip, 2½″ × 8½″*

From blue paisley fabric cut:

- *1 B strip, 2½″ × 4½″*
- *1 C strip, 2½″ × 6½″*
- *1 D strip, 2½″ × 8½″*
- *1 E strip, 2½″ × 10½″*

From ecru fabric cut:

- *2 K strips, each 2½″ × 24½″*
- *4 L strips, each 2½″ × 34½″*

Apron

1. Make one blue pieced log cabin block, as you did for the quilt (see Quilt instructions, steps 1–7).

2. Stitch the 5 K (2½″ × 24½″) strips (2 ecru, 3 red) together along their long sides, alternating colors, as shown in Figure 7–13d, to make the central unit. Set it aside.

3. To make the long side unit (Fig. 7–13b), stitch two red L strips (2½″ × 34½″) alternating with two ecru L strips, along their long sides.

4. Repeat Step 3 with the remaining 4 L strips for the second long side unit (Fig. 7–13c).

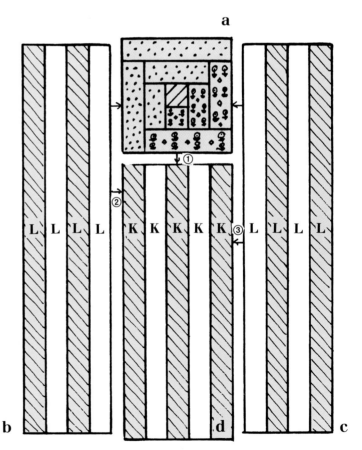

*7–13 Construction diagram for apron. **a,** pieced square; **b and c,** long side units; **d,** central unit. Circled numbers indicate order of piecing.*

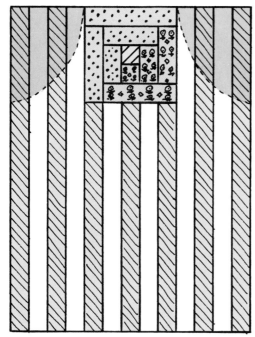

7–14 Cutting armhole curves. Discard shaded areas.

5. Assemble all the units as shown in the construction diagram (Fig. 7–13). Press the unit.

6. Cut armhole curves on the apron sides, as shown in Figure 7–14, using the armhole cutting guide (Fig. 7–15), and aligning the top edge of the guide with the top edge of the apron piece and the side edge of the guide with the side edge of the apron piece. (Reverse the cutting guide for the left armhole.)

7. Place the apron front on the apron backing piece (28″ × 35″), with right sides of material together. With a seam allowance of ¼″, stitch along the apron top, down the sides, and across the bottom (see Fig. 7–16). Do not stitch the armhole areas. Trim away the excess backing, using the apron front as a guide. Clip the seam allowance at the curves, trim the corners of the seam allowance, and turn the apron right-side out.

8. Align the layers of the raw armhole edges and baste the layers together, close to the edges.

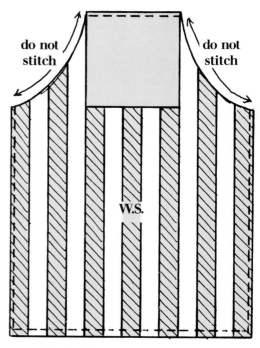

7–16 Dashed lines indicate stitching lines (done with right sides of fabric facing together). Leave armhole curves unstitched.

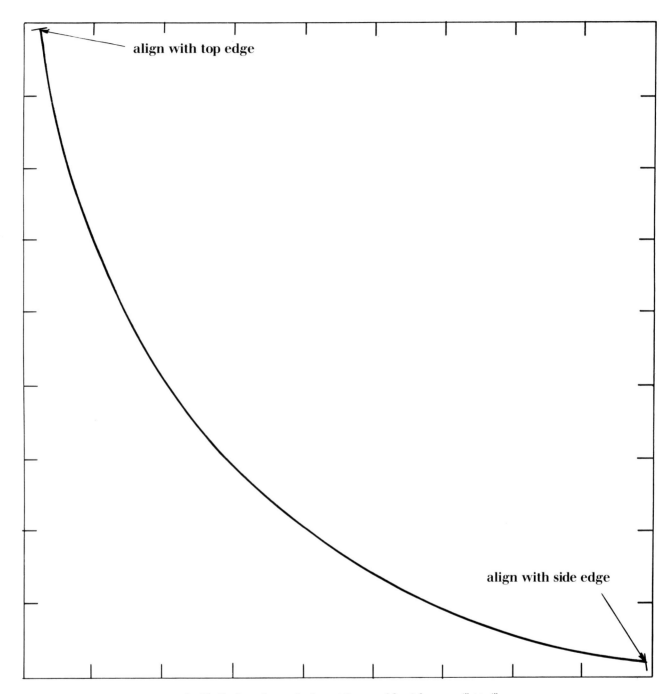

7–15 *Reduced armhole cutting guide. 1 box = 1" × 1".*

9. Cut the blue binding into two equal lengths. Mark the center of each length, and pin one on the center front of each armhole. Baste the binding to the armhole on the front of the apron, with raw edges of apron and binding aligned, leaving the tails of the binding hanging off either end; these will become the apron neck and waist ties (Fig. 7–17).

10. Starting at the end of one tie, fold in the raw end and stitch it down. Then fold the binding in half lengthwise, and stitch it closed along its length, close to the edges, until you reach the armhole edge. As you close the binding at the armhole, enclose the raw armhole edges inside the binding. Then continue stitching down the remaining folded length of the other end of the binding to finish the tie; at the end, tuck the raw edge of the binding in and stitch it. Repeat this for the second side of the apron.

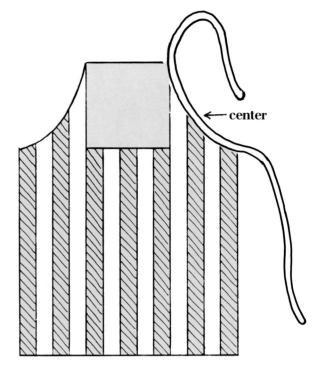

← center

7–17 Center the length of the binding on the armhole center, and baste the binding to the right side of the armhole.

Ice Cream Cone Quilt

Make each scoop a different flavor in this scrap-basket project. Finished size of quilt: 40″ × 49″ (block size: 8″ × 11″).

Materials Required

- *1 yard white broadcloth*
- *½ yard each light green, yellow, bright pink, and light purple print fabrics (for borders)*
- *Brown and tan scraps totalling ½ yard*
- *Scraps of pastel colors totalling ⅔ yard*
- *42″ × 51″ piece of backing fabric*
- *42″ × 51″ piece of quilt batting*
- *1 yard fusible transfer webbing*
- *Sewing and embroidery threads to match each fabric*
- *6 yards of white ½″ extra-wide double-fold bias binding (unfolded width = 2″)*

Directions

Note: All measurements include ¼″ seam allowances, except for appliqué patterns. Piecing is done with right sides of fabric facing.

1. From the white fabric, cut nine 8½″ × 11½″ rectangles. Fold each rectangle in half lengthwise and press it to mark the centerline.

2. Trace 9 ice cream cones and 9 scoops (Fig. 8–2) onto fusible webbing, and cut them out. Fuse the cones to the brown and tan pieces of scrap yardage. Fuse the scoops to the various shades of scrap pastel fabric. Cut out the cones and scoops, and fuse one complete ice cream cone to the center of each white rectangle (see photo). The cone's point should be on the rectangle's centerline. Machine-appliqué the pieces in place with matching threads and a medium-width machine satin stitch.

3. Stitch the ice cream cone blocks together on their long sides in 3 rows of 3 blocks each. Stitch the 3 rows together to make the quilt center (see Fig. 8–1). Press.

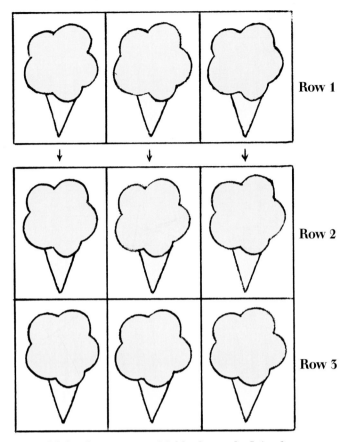

Row 1

Row 2

Row 3

8–1 Make three rows of 3 blocks each. Join the three rows together to form the center portion of the quilt.

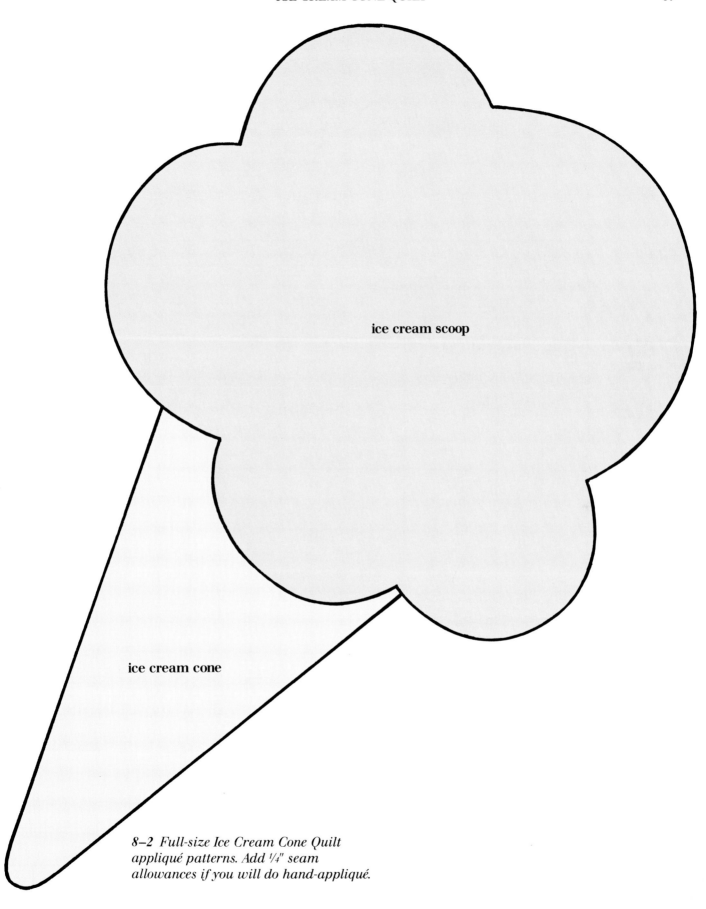

ice cream scoop

ice cream cone

8–2 Full-size Ice Cream Cone Quilt appliqué patterns. Add ¼" seam allowances if you will do hand-appliqué.

4. Cut sixteen 2½″ I squares from various shades of brown and tan for the border corner blocks (see photo and Fig. 8–3).

5. Cut the borders as indicated in the border cutting guide table.

6. Take the 2½″ × 33½″ light green border strips (A strips). Stitch them to the long sides of the quilt center (Fig. 8–3).

7. Take the 2½″ × 24½″ light green border strips (B strips). Stitch a tan or brown I square to the short ends of each B strip.

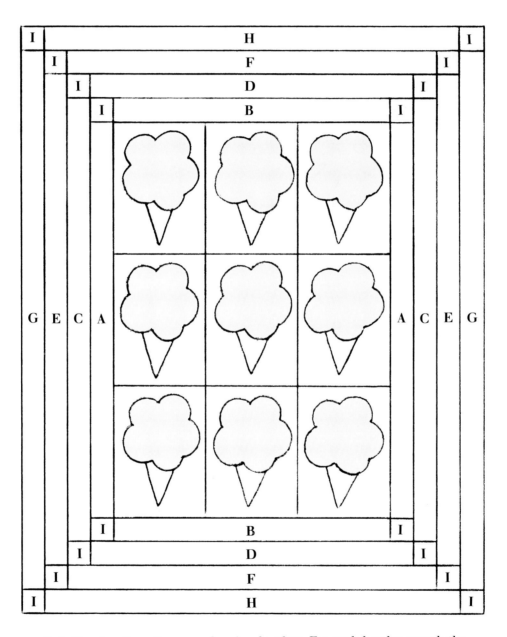

8–3 Construction diagram showing borders. For each border, attach the side strips first; then piece and attach the top and bottom borders.

8. Stitch the border units made in Step 7 to the top and bottom of the unit made in Step 6 (Fig. 8–3). Press.

9. For the yellow, light red, and light purple borders, repeat the process of joining the long side borders, making the top and bottom border units, and then joining the border units to the top and bottom of the quilt (see Fig. 8–3 and the color photo for reference). Each short border has tan or brown I squares attached to its ends.

Border Cutting Guide for Quilt

Fabric Color	Border	Size of strips (cut 2 of each)
Light green print	Inner	2½″ × 33½″ (A) 2½″ × 24½″ (B)
Yellow print	Second	2½″ × 37½″ (C) 2½″ × 28½″ (D)
Light red print	Third	2½″ × 41½″ (E) 2½″ × 32½″ (F)
Light purple print (lilac)	Outer	2½″ × 45½″ (G) 2½″ × 36½″ (H)

10. Lay the backing face-down on your work surface. Center the quilt batting over the backing. Center the quilt top, face-up, over the batting. Pin-baste the layers together. Machine-quilt along the seamlines, around each appliqué, and again ¼″ from the outside edges of the appliqués. Quilt down the centers of each border strip.

11. Baste around the edges of the quilt top. Trim away the excess batting and backing, and bind the quilt with the white binding (see the General Directions chapter for binding information).

Child's Beach Tote

This tote is large enough to hold all of your beach essentials. It's designed for kids, but plenty of adults will want one as well. Finished size: 16″ × 16″, excluding handles.

Materials Required

- *1 yard red fabric with dots*
- *10½″ square of turquoise fabric*
- *Scraps of white, red, yellow, green, and purple fabrics*
- *Sewing and embroidery threads to match the fabrics*
- *2 squares, each 16″ × 16″, of fusible or regular fleece*
- *2 strips, each 2″ × 18″, of fusible or regular fleece*
- *½ yard fusible transfer webbing*
- *45″ length of white medium rickrack*
- *Black embroidery floss*

Directions

Overview: The outer bag of the tote and the lining are made as two separate units and then are joined. Piecing is done with ¼″ seam allowances and right sides of fabric facing.

1. Trace the reversed appliqué pattern pieces from Figure 9–1 onto the back of the fusible webbing and cut them out. Fuse the webbing pieces to the wrong sides of fabrics, as follows: Fuse the horse's body to the white fabric scrap. Fuse the mane, nose, tail, and saddle strap to red fabric scraps. Fuse two dots to purple fabric and 3 dots to the green scrap fabric. Fuse the saddle to yellow scrap fabric. Cut out all the fused pieces.

2. With chalk or light blue washable pencil, transfer the eye, mouth, and nose markings to the white fabric horse.

3. Fuse the appliqués onto the white horse and, with the horse centered on the turquoise square, fuse the horse to the square. See the photo for reference.

Machine-appliqué the pieces in place, using thread that matches each piece.

4. From the red dotted fabric, cut 2 strips, each 3½″ × 10½″. With right sides of the fabric facing, stitch one strip to the top of the turquoise block and one to the bottom of the turquoise block.

5. Cut two 3½″ × 16½″ strips from the red dotted fabric, and stitch them to the sides of the unit made in Step 4. Press. This will be the front of the bag.

6. Cut three 16½″ squares from the dotted red fabric. One will be used for the back of the outer bag and two will become the lining of the tote bag.

7. To make the outer bag's back, fuse or baste one 16½″ fleece square to the wrong side of one of the red squares cut in Step 6. Fuse or baste the remaining fleece square to the wrong side of the appliquéd square to make the outside front.

8. On the appliquéd square unit, stitch white rickrack around the appliquéd turquoise square, covering the seamlines; tuck the raw edges of the rickrack under at the ends. (See photo for position of rickrack.)

9. Stitch the two units made in Step 7, the outer bag back and the outer bag front, together with right sides facing, leaving the top edge of the unit unstitched.

10. Clip the corners of the seam allowances at the bottoms of the resulting outer bag (Fig. 9–2), but don't turn it right-side out yet. Press the seam allowances open.

11. To pleat the outer bag bottom so it will stand, align the left side seam with the bottom seam. Mark a line exactly 1″ from the resulting point to form a triangle (see Fig. 9–3). Stitch along the marked line by machine. Stitch in the same way at the other corner of the outer bag bottom. Turn the outer bag right-side out.

12. Stitch the two remaining red squares (cut in Step 9) together with right sides facing (as

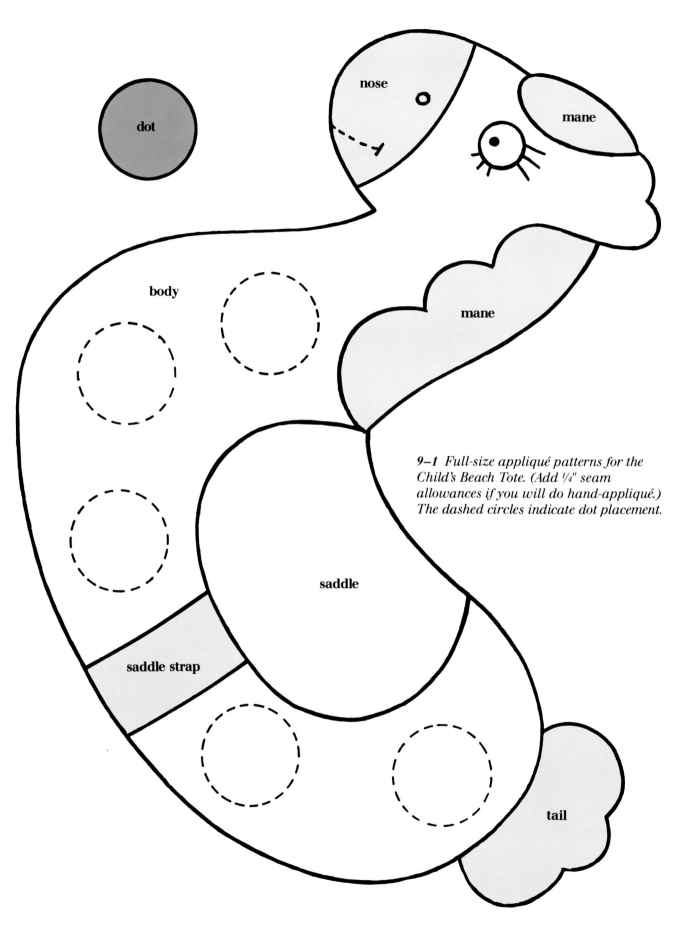

dot

nose

mane

mane

body

saddle

9–1 *Full-size appliqué patterns for the Child's Beach Tote. (Add ¼″ seam allowances if you will do hand-appliqué.) The dashed circles indicate dot placement.*

saddle strap

tail

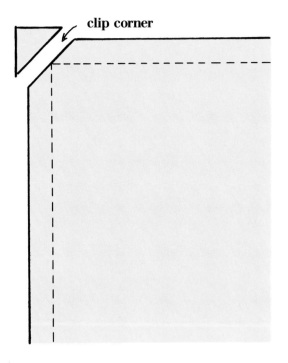

clip corner

9–2 *Clip the corners from the seam allowances at the bottom close to, but not cutting into, the seamline.*

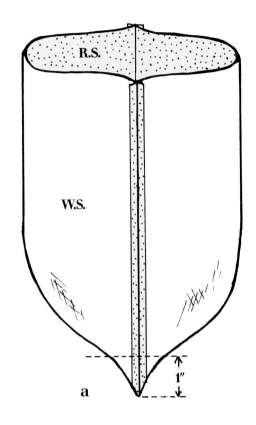

R.S.

W.S.

a

1″

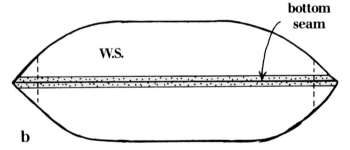

bottom seam

W.S.

b

9–3 *Pleating the corners of the bag.* **a:** *After pressing the side seams open, align the side seam with the bottom seam, mark a line 1″ from the point of the corner, and stitch.* **b:** *Bottom view of the bag, showing stitched pleating lines (dashed lines).*

in steps 9 and 10), and pleat them as you did for the outer bag (see Step 11). This forms the lining bag.

13. Cut two strips, each 5″ × 18″, from the dotted red fabric. They will become handles.

14. Fuse or baste one of the 2″ × 18″ fleece strips down the center of each red strip cut in Step 13, on the wrong side of the fabric (Fig. 9–4a). Fold over one long edge on each fabric strip to partially cover the fleece (Fig. 9–4b, right). Press it in place. Fold under ¼″ to the wrong side of the fabric on the remaining long side of each red strip (Fig. 9–4b, left). Then fold the same long side over the center of the strip, covering the raw edge of the first side of the strip; the ¼″ fold should be tucked under (Fig. 9–4c). Stitch the material in place.

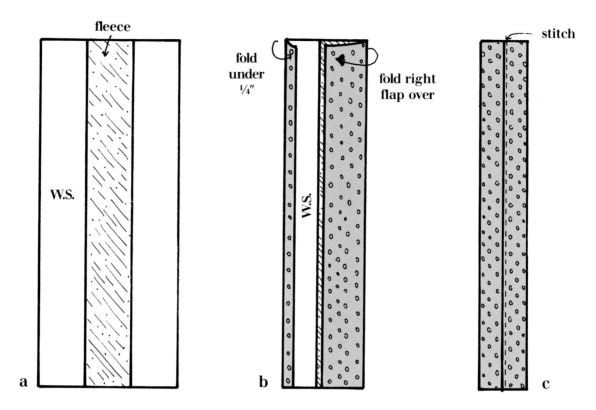

9–4 *Making a handle.* **a:** *Attach the fleece.* **b:** *Fold the right flap of fabric over to cover the fleece. Fold a ¼" hem in on the left side and press it.* **c:** *Fold the left flap over and stitch it in place close to the fold.*

15. Repeat Step 14 to make the second handle.

16. Baste one handle to the outside of the front of the outer bag, 3" from the side seams (Fig. 9–5). The raw edges of the handles should align with the raw edge of the outer bag's top (Fig. 9–5). Repeat this process for the second handle on the back of the outer bag.

17. Place the outer bag inside the lining bag with right sides together, align the seams, and baste and stitch them together along the top edge with ¼" seam allowance, leaving a 3" opening in the un-appliquéd side through which to turn the bag.

18. Turn the bag right-side out. Push the lining bag into the outside bag and press the entire bag. Sew up the remaining 3" opening. Then stitch around the top of the bag, close to the edge, to keep the layers from shifting.

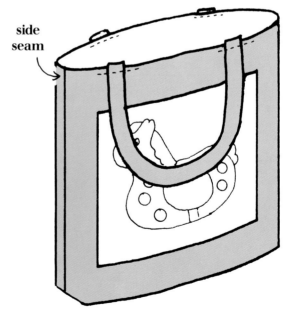

9–5 *Basting a handle to the outer bag.*

Sailboat Pillows

You need not live by the sea to enjoy these! Slip them onto your favorite bench or chair and you'll almost be able to smell that salty ocean air! Finished size of each pillow: 16″ × 16″.

Materials Required for Two Pillows

- *¾ yard each of blue cotton duck and red cotton duck, or other heavy cotton fabric*

- *½ yard white cotton duck*

- *1 yard fusible transfer webbing*

- *All-purpose threads to match the fabrics*

- *Machine embroidery threads to match the fabrics*

- *3 yards of white piping*

- *2 pillow forms, each 16″ × 16″*

- *6 plastic rings, ¾″ in diameter (from a knitting supply shop)*

Directions

Note: All measurements, except appliqué patterns, include ¼″ seam allowances.

1. Enlarge the sailboat pattern from Figure 10–1 (see enlarging tips in the General Directions chapter). Trace two reversed sailboats and sails onto the paper backing of fusible webbing, and cut out the parts from the webbing.

2. Cut 16½″ squares, two from red and two from blue fabric. Set one blue and one red square aside for the pillow backings.

3. Fuse one webbing boat hull to the wrong side of the remaining red fabric, and fuse one webbing boat hull to the wrong side of the remaining blue fabric, and cut them out of the fabric.

4. Fuse 2 webbing hull bottoms and 2 sets of webbing sails to the back of the white fabric, and cut them out of the fabric. Transfer the sail markings (see Fig. 10–1) to the right sides of the sails.

5. Lightly draw the enlarged sailboat pattern on the outside of one red and one blue square with light blue washable pencil or chalk, centering the pattern on the square.

6. Fuse the sailboat fabric pieces in place on the red and blue squares (see photo).

7. Machine appliqué the pieces in place with machine embroidery threads.

8. Stitch 3 rings to each hull (see photo), using blue all-purpose thread for the red hull and red all-purpose thread for the blue hull. Satin-stitch the sail details with white thread.

9. Using a ¼″ seam allowance and white all-purpose thread, baste white piping around the edges of the appliquéd squares on the right side of the fabric. The raw edges of the piping should align with the raw edges of the square. See the section on piping in the General Directions chapter for more details.

10. With right sides of the material together, stitch a blue backing square to a red appliquéd sailboat square, following the basting lines used for the piping; stitch a red backing square to a blue appliquéd sailboat square in the same way. Leave the bottom edges of the pillow covers open, so they can be turned right-side out.

11. Clip the corners of the seam allowances, and turn the pillow covers right-side out. Insert the pillow forms and stitch the openings closed with threads that match the backings.

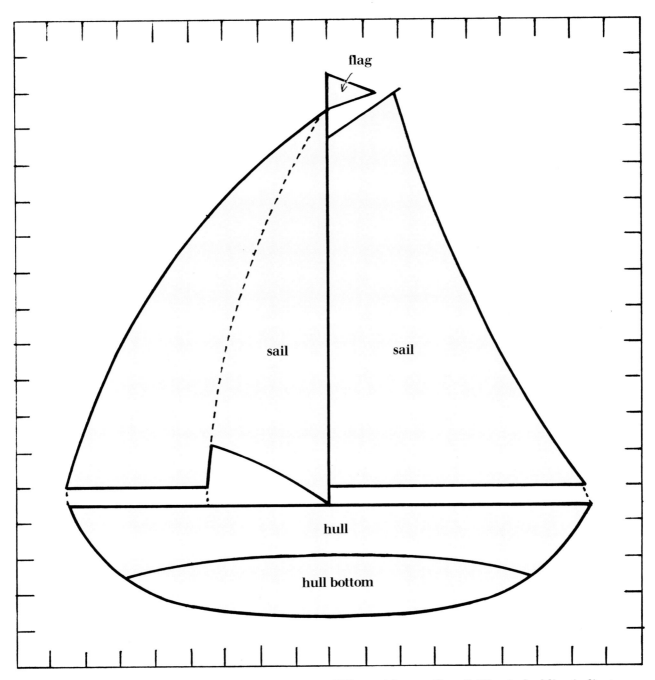

10–1 *Reduced appliqué pattern for the Sailboat Pillows. 1 box = 1" × 1". The dashed line indicates satin-stitched details. (If you will do hand appliqué, add ¼" allowance around each piece, after enlarging the pattern.)*

Autumn's Colorful Harvest

Back-to-School Lunch Sacks

Even the pickiest of eaters will enjoy eating lunch out of these, and the sacks are machine-washable! Make several to give as gifts. Finished size of sack: 10″ × 12″.

Materials Required for Two Sacks

* *2 pieces of white fabric, each 6⅜″ × 8½″ (one piece for each bag)*

* *1 yard washable print fabric for borders, straps, and lining (Each sack requires ½ yard.)*

* *Scraps of red and green fabric for the apple*

* *Scraps of red, green, yellow, and tan for the pizza*

* *1 yard fusible or sew-in fleece*

* *Threads to match the fabrics, plus black thread and brown thread*

* *⅓ yard fusible transfer webbing*

Directions for One Sack

Overview: The outer bag of the sack and the lining are made as two separate units and then are joined. *Note:* All measurements, except appliqué patterns, include ¼″ seam allowances.

1. Place a 6⅜″ × 8½″ white rectangle of fabric directly over the full-size appliqué pattern you have chosen (Fig. 11–1 or 11–2). With light blue pencil, trace the lettering onto the fabric, and lightly trace the outline of the appliqué pattern.

2. Trace the reversed appliqué pieces onto the back of fusible webbing, and cut them out of the webbing.

3. Fuse the webbing pieces to the scrap fabrics, referring to the color photo for the color of each piece. Cut out the appliqué pieces from their respective fabrics. For the pizza appliqué, fuse the small appliqué pieces onto the large red piece.

4. Fuse the appliqué shapes onto the white fabric rectangle, following the outline you traced in Step 1 for position.

5. Machine-appliqué the pieces in place (see the section on machine appliqué in the General Directions chapter for reference). Use thread to match each individual appliqué piece.

6. Machine satin-stitch along the letter outlines on the white rectangle, using black thread. For the apple in Fig. 11–1, machine satin-stitch the stem with brown thread.

7. For the side borders of the sack front, cut 2 strips, 2½″ × 8½″ each, from the print fabric of your choice; stitch one strip to each long side of the appliquéd white rectangle, with right sides of material facing and ¼″ seam allowance.

8. For the top and bottom borders, cut 2 strips, 2½″ × 10½″ each, from the same printed fabric as the side borders, and sew them to the top and bottom of the unit made in Step 7, with right sides of material facing. This completes the outer bag front. Press.

9. Fuse or baste a 10½″ × 12½″ piece of fleece to the wrong side of the completed outer bag front.

10. Cut three 10½″ × 12½″ rectangles from the same printed material you used for the borders, and fuse or baste a 10½″ × 12½″ piece of fleece to the wrong side of one of them. This will become the back of the outer bag. (The unfleeced rectangles will become the lining.)

11. With right sides of material facing, stitch the outer bag front (made in Step 8) to the outer bag back (made in Step 10), with ¼″ seam allowance; leave the top side unstitched, however. This unit is the outer bag. Do not turn it right-side out.

12. Stitch the two remaining unfleeced lining pieces, cut in Step 10, together along 3 sides, with ¼″ seam allowance and right sides of material facing, leaving one short side open. This makes the lining bag. Clip the corners of the seam allowances at the bottom of the lining bag. (Fig. 11–3), but don't turn it right-side out.

13. To pleat the bottom corners of the lining bag, so that it will be able to stand, align the left side seam with the bottom seam, and fold the corner of the bottom up in a triangle (see Fig. 11–4) (the lining bag is still facing

11–1 *Full-size Apple Lunch Sack pattern. The dashed line is the seamline; the outer line is the cutting line. (For hand appliqué, add ¼" seam allowance around the apple and the leaf when cutting.)*

11–2 *Full-size Pizza Lunch Sack pattern. The dashed line is the seamline; the outer line is the cutting line. (For hand appliqué, add ¼″ seam allowance around each of the pizza pieces when cutting.)*

wrong-side out). Stitch across the resulting triangle 1″ down from its point. Repeat this at the other bottom corner of the lining bag. Set the lining bag aside.

14. Pleat the bottom corners of the outer bag, formed in Step 11, as you did with the lining bag. Set it aside.

15. For handles, cut 2 strips, 3″ × 14½″ each, from the same print you used earlier.

16. To complete the handles, take the strips cut in Step 15, fold each strip in half lengthwise, with right sides of material together, and stitch the strip along two sides, ¼″ from the raw edges; leave one short side open for turning. Turn the handles right-side out.

17. Center the seamline along the length of the strip for each handle, and press it.

18. Baste one handle to the right side of the outer bag front (see Fig. 11–5); its ends should be 2″ in from the side seams. The raw edges of the handles should align with the raw edge of the outer bag's top. Repeat this process for the second handle.

19. Place the outer bag inside the lining bag with right sides together, align the side seams, and baste and stitch the bags together along the top edge with ¼″ seam allowance, leaving a 3″ opening on the un-appliquéd side through which to turn the bag.

20. Turn the bag right-side out. Push the lining into the outer bag and press the entire bag. Sew up the remaining 3″ opening. Stitch around the top of the bag with matching thread, close to the edge, to keep the layers from shifting.

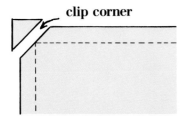

clip corner

11–3 Clip the corners of the seam allowances at the bottom close to, but not cutting into, the seamline.

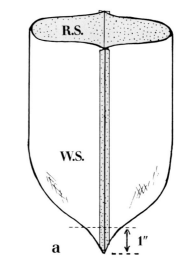

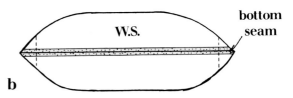

*11–4 Pleating the corner of the bag. **a:** After pressing the side seams open, align the side seam with the bottom seam, mark a line 1″ from the point of the corner, and stitch. **b:** Bottom view of the bag, showing stitched pleating lines (dashed lines).*

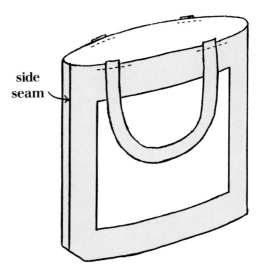

11–5 Basting the handle to the outer bag.

Quilted Backgammon Board

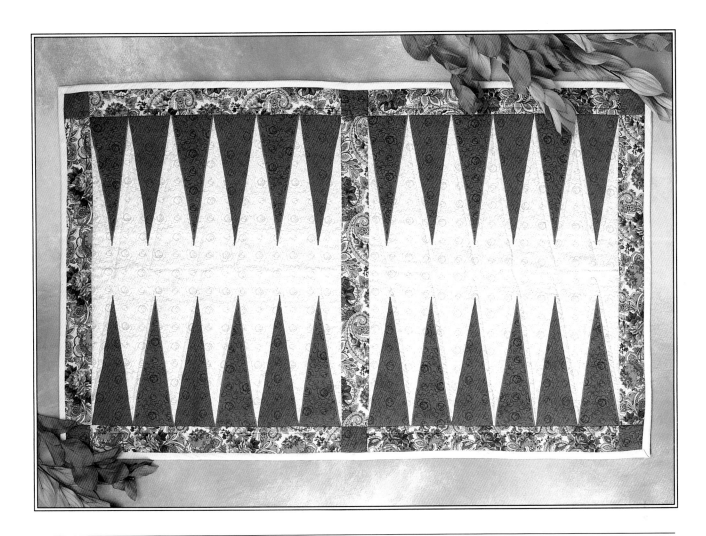

Someone special would surely love to receive this as a gift! Stitch it in his or her favorite colors to make it truly special! (The colors given in the materials list are the ones used in the model.) Finished size: 25″ × 42″.

Materials Required

- *½ yard tan print fabric*
- *⅓ yard each rust print fabric and teal print fabric*
- *⅓ yard floral print for border, with colors that coordinate with the other fabrics*
- *27" × 44" piece of fabric for the backing*
- *27" × 44" piece of fleece or quilt batting*
- *Sewing and quilting threads to match fabrics*
- *⅔ yard fusible transfer webbing*
- *4 yards light tan (ecru) ½" extra-wide double-folded bias binding (unfolded width = 2")*

Directions

Note: ¼" seam allowances are included in all measurements, unless noted.

1. Cut two 18½" × 21½" rectangles from the tan print fabric.

2. Trace the triangle (Figure 12–1) onto cardboard or other template material and cut it out.

3. Trace 24 triangles with your triangle template onto fusible webbing, and cut them out of the webbing.

4. Fuse 12 of the webbing triangles to the back of the rust print fabric; fuse the remaining 12 to the back of the teal print fabric. Cut out the triangles from the fabrics. Referring to Figure 12–2, fuse the triangles to the tan rectangles cut in Step 1, alternating teal and rust triangles, as shown in the color

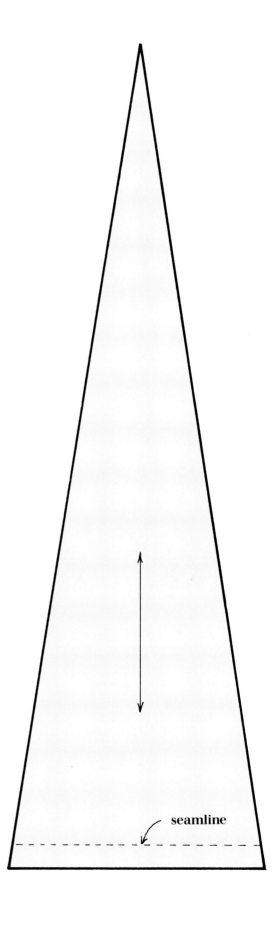

seamline

***12–1** Full-size appliqué pattern for the backgammon board. The arrow indicates the straight grain of the fabric. Machine-appliqué the triangles only along the two long sides when attaching them. The short (bottom) side has ¼" seam allowance; its edge will become part of the seam allowance. The long sides have no seam allowance. (If you will do hand appliqué, add ¼" seam allowances to the long sides before cutting the triangles).*

photo. Align the bottom (short) sides of the triangles with the raw edges of the rectangles, and make sure that the outermost triangles don't extend into the ¼″ seam allowances at the sides.

5. Machine-appliqué each triangle in place with thread that matches the color of the appliquéd piece. Press.

6. From the floral print fabric, cut 3 strips, each 21½″ × 2½″ (A strips).

7. Referring to Figure 12–3, join the A strips to the appliquéd tan rectangles with right sides of material facing and ¼″ seam allowances. Press.

8. From the floral print cut 4 strips, each 18½″ × 2½″ (B strips). Cut 3 C squares 2½″ × 2½″ each, from rust print fabric and 3 C squares the same size from teal print fabric.

9. Referring to Figure 12–3 and the color photo, stitch the C squares to the short sides of the floral print B strips to make two long border rows, alternating colors of the C squares, as shown in the photo.

10. With right sides of material facing and ¼″ seam allowances, join each row made in Step 9 to a long side of the central backgammon board unit, as shown in Figure 12–3. This completes the quilt top of the backgammon board.

11. Lay the backing fabric (27″ × 44″) face-down on your work surface. Center the fleece or batting over the backing, and center the backgammon board top, face-up, over the fleece.

12. Pin-baste or baste the layers together. Quilt the layers along all seamlines and also ¼″ away from the seamlines, or in another pattern you like.

13. Baste through all three layers near to the edges of the backgammon board top to secure them. Trim away the excess batting and backing. Bind the board with the light tan binding (see the General Directions chapter for binding information).

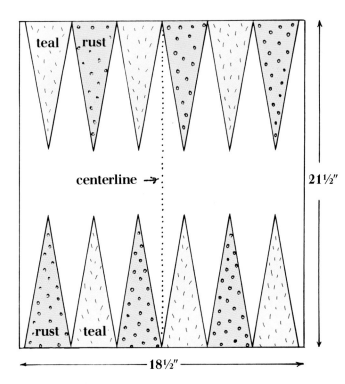

12–2 Construction diagram for the backgammon board. Place 3 triangles along each side of the centerline for each row of triangles. Be sure the outermost triangles do not extend into the ¼″ side seam allowances.

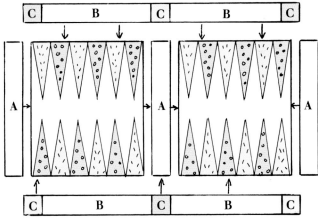

12–3 Join the A strips to the appliquéd tan rectangles. Then make the long border rows, and join the long border rows to the unit.

Petrified Pumpkin Treat Bag

This pumpkin looks as if he's been frightened by all the ghosts and goblins that have shown up on the doorstep! He's sure to please your trick-or-treaters. Finished size of treat bag: Approximately 14″ × 14″, excluding handles.

Materials Required

- *⅔ yard orange-and-yellow print fabric*
- *½ yard each solid black fabric, orange pin-dot fabric, and black-and-orange print fabric*
- *Scraps of yellow fabric and green fabric*
- *½ yard fusible transfer webbing*
- *Machine embroidery threads to match the fabrics*
- *Black and orange all-purpose threads*
- *2 glue-on moving eyes, 1″ in diameter*
- *10″ scrap of ¼″-wide yellow satin ribbon*

Directions

Overview: The outer bag and the lining are made as two separate units and then are joined. *Note:* except for the appliqués, all measurements include ¼″ seam allowances.

1. Cut four 14½″ squares from the orange-and-yellow print fabric. From the black-and-orange print, cut 2 handle strips, each 3″ × 18″. Cut a 10½″ square from the solid black fabric. The black square will be the background behind the pumpkin.

2. From Figure 13–1, trace out the full pattern onto tracing paper (see the General Directions chapter for tracing a half-pattern). Then trace the reversed pumpkin appliqué pieces onto the paper side of fusible webbing.

3. Cut out the entire pumpkin shape in one piece; also cut the eye sockets, stem, nose, and mouth from the webbing.

4. Fuse the webbing pumpkin to the orange pin-dot fabric. Fuse the webbing stem to the green fabric; fuse the eye sockets, nose, and mouth to the yellow fabric. (All are fused to the wrong sides of the fabrics.)

5. Cut out the shapes fused in Step 4 from the fabrics.

6. Transfer all the appliqué lines and the dotted lines shown in Figure 13–1 to the right side of the orange pin-dot pumpkin, using washable light blue pencil. Fuse the yellow facial features in place on the pumpkin.

7. Fold the black square that you cut in Step 1 in half, and press it so it has a centerline. Fuse the pumpkin and its stem to the black square, matching the centerline of the pumpkin to the centerline of the black square, with the pumpkin centered from top to bottom on the square.

8. Machine-appliqué all the pieces in place, using machine embroidery thread that matches the color of each respective piece. Machine satin-stitch down the "vein" lines of the pumpkin in red. Stop stitching when you come to an appliqué, and continue stitching the vein line beyond the appliqué, where necessary.

9. Turn under ¼″ to the back on all sides of the black square. Using black all-purpose thread, hand-appliqué the black square to the center of one of the 14½″ orange squares you cut in Step 1. Set it aside for now. If you prefer to machine-appliqué the black square in place, trim off the ¼″ seam allowance around the black square on all 4 sides and satin-stitch it to the center of the orange square with black thread.

10. For handles, fold each precut black-and-orange handle strip (from Step 1) in half lengthwise, with right sides together. Using all-purpose thread, stitch closed the long raw edge of each handle, using a ¼″ seam allowance (leave the ends open). Turn the handles right-side out. Press them flat and baste them across their short ends. Set them aside.

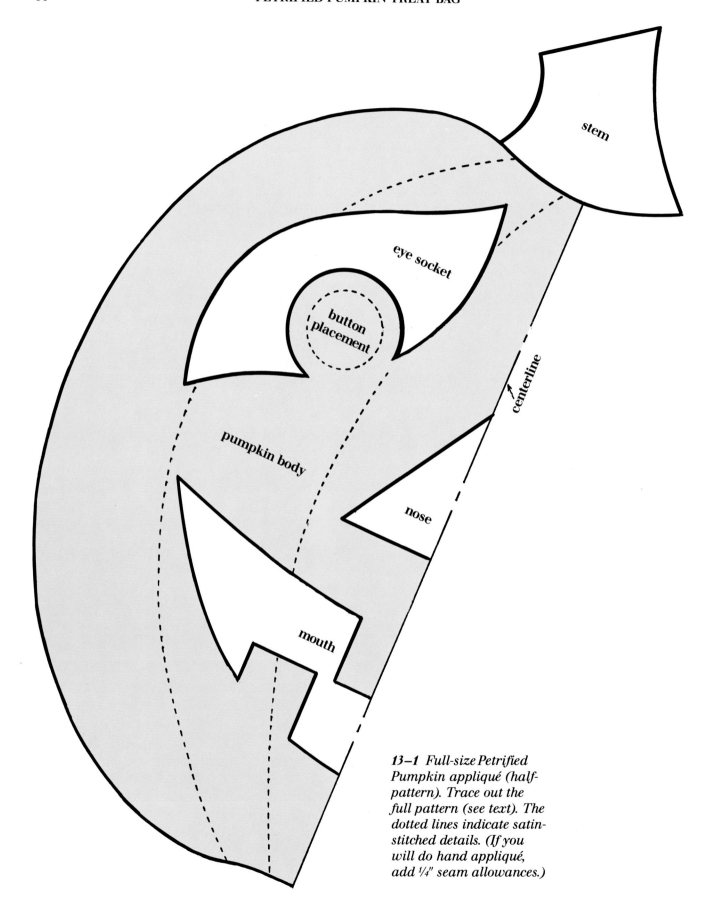

13–1 Full-size Petrified Pumpkin appliqué (half-pattern). Trace out the full pattern (see text). The dotted lines indicate satin-stitched details. (If you will do hand appliqué, add ¼" seam allowances.)

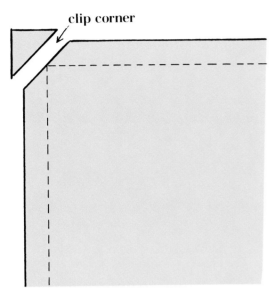

13–2 *Clip corners from the seam allowance at the bottom close to, but not cutting into, the seamline of the bag.*

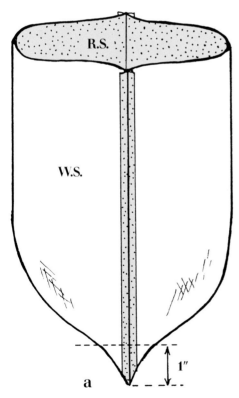

a

13–3 *Pleating the corners of the bag. a: After pressing the side seams open, align the side seam with the bottom seam, mark a line 1″ from the point of the corner, and stitch. b: Bottom view of the bag, showing stitched pleating lines (dashed lines).*

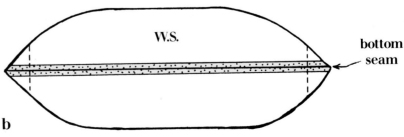

b

11. Using a ¼″ seam allowance and orange all-purpose thread, take two of the 14½″ (unappliquéd) orange-and-yellow squares cut in Step 1. With right sides together, stitch them together around two long sides and the bottom to make the lining of the bag. Clip the corners of the seam allowances (Fig. 13–2) at the bottom of the bag. Do not turn it right-side out.

12. To pleat the bottom corners of the lining bag, so that it will be able to stand, align the left side seam with the bottom seam, and fold the corner of the bottom up in a triangle (see Fig. 13–3) on the wrong side of the material. Stitch across the resulting triangle 1″ down from its point. Repeat this at the other bottom corner of the lining bag. Set it aside.

13. With right sides of material facing and ¼″ seam allowance, stitch the remaining orange square cut in Step 1 to the appliquéd square made in Step 9; stitch around 3 sides, leaving the top side open. This forms the outer bag. Clip the corners of the seam allowances as you did in Step 11. Pleat the corners of the outer bag as you did for the lining bag (Step 12). Turn the outer bag right-side out.

14. Baste one handle to the right side of the outer bag front (see Fig. 13–4); its ends

should be 3″ in from the side seams (Fig. 13–4). The raw edges of the handles should align with the raw edge of the outer bag's top. Repeat this process for the second handle.

15. Place the outer bag inside the lining bag with right sides together, align the seams, and baste and stitch the bags together along the top edge with ¼″ seam allowance, leaving a 3″ opening in the un-appliquéd side through which to turn the bag.

16. Turn the bag right-side out. Push the lining bag into the outside bag, and press the entire bag. Sew up the remaining 3″ opening. Then stitch around the top of the bag, close to the edge, to keep the layers from shifting.

17. Glue movable eyes to the pumpkin, as indicated on Figure 13–1, using fabric glue or a hot glue gun. Tie the yellow ribbon into a bow and tack it in place at the center of the stem to complete the project.

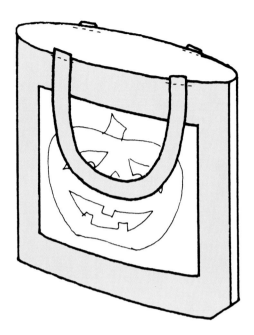

13–4 Basting a handle to the outer bag.

Boo Banner

Surprise your favorite trick-or-treater with this easy-to-make project. Finished size of banner: 16″ × 38″.

Materials Required

- *½ yard each of black fabric and orange fabric*
- *⅓ yard each of yellow fabric and white fabric*
- *18″ × 40″ piece of fabric for backing*
- *18″ × 40″ piece of fleece or quilt batting*
- *½ yard fusible transfer webbing*
- *Sewing and quilting threads to match fabrics*
- *⅓ yard ¼″-wide yellow satin ribbon*
- *Black embroidery floss*
- *4 yards black ½″ extra-wide double-fold binding (unfolded width = 2″)*

Directions

Note: All block and border measurements include ¼″ seam allowances. The appliqué patterns do not include seam allowances, as they are designed for machine appliqué. Add ¼″ seam allowance around each appliqué pattern if you will do hand appliqué, and see General Directions for hand appliqué.

1. Trace letters BOO (Fig. 14–2, 14–3) onto tracing paper. Turn the tracing paper over so that the letters are reversed, and trace the letters onto the back of the fusible webbing.

2. Cut out the webbing letters and fuse them onto the wrong side of the orange fabric; then cut them out of the fabric. The webbing will be adhered to the backs of the letters.

3. Trace the ghost (Figure 14–4) onto tracing paper. Turn it over to reverse it and trace it three times onto the back of the fusible webbing. Cut out the webbing ghosts and fuse them to the back of the white fabric. From Figure 14–4, trace the eye markings to the right side of the fabric for each ghost, using washable light-blue pencil. Cut out the appliqué ghosts from the white fabric.

4. From black fabric, cut three 10½″ squares.

5. Fold each square in half and press it to mark the centerline. Fuse one letter and one ghost to each black square as shown.

6. Appliqué the ghosts and letters to the black blocks, using threads that match the fabrics.

7. Hand-embroider the ghosts' eyes, using 3 strands of black embroidery floss, in satin stitch.

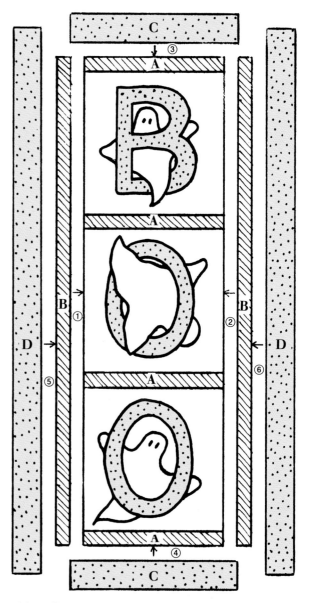

14–1 *Construction diagram for the Boo Banner. Circled numbers indicate order of piecing.*

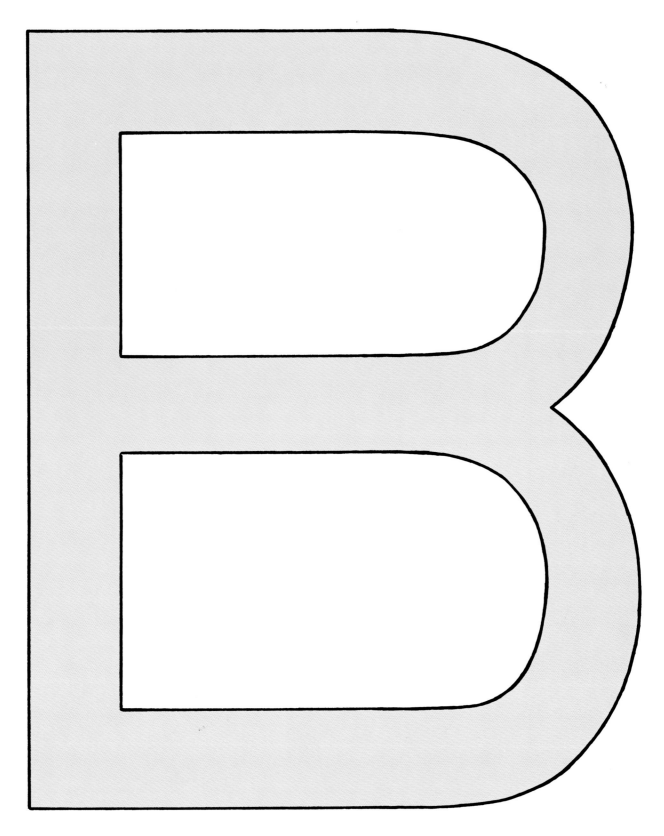

14–2 *Full-size appliqué pattern for the Boo Banner. (For hand appliqué add ¼″ seam allowances.) Cut 1.*

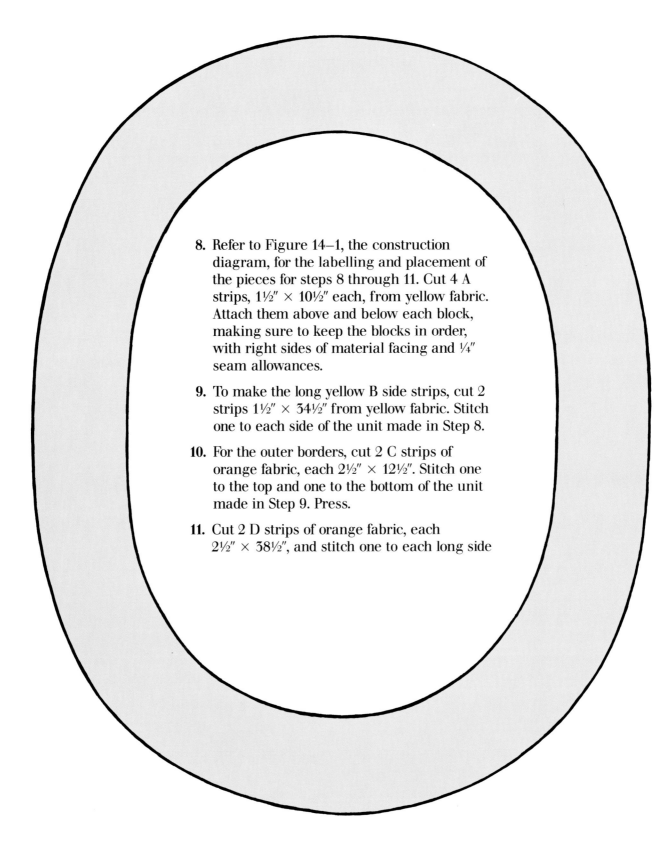

8. Refer to Figure 14–1, the construction diagram, for the labelling and placement of the pieces for steps 8 through 11. Cut 4 A strips, 1½″ × 10½″ each, from yellow fabric. Attach them above and below each block, making sure to keep the blocks in order, with right sides of material facing and ¼″ seam allowances.

9. To make the long yellow B side strips, cut 2 strips 1½″ × 34½″ from yellow fabric. Stitch one to each side of the unit made in Step 8.

10. For the outer borders, cut 2 C strips of orange fabric, each 2½″ × 12½″. Stitch one to the top and one to the bottom of the unit made in Step 9. Press.

11. Cut 2 D strips of orange fabric, each 2½″ × 38½″, and stitch one to each long side

14–3 Full-size appliqué pattern for the Boo Banner. Cut 2. (For hand appliqué, add ¼″ seam allowances.)

14–4 Full-size ghost appliqué pattern for Boo Banner. Satin-stitch the eyes (black dots). For hand appliqué, add ¼″ seam allowances.

of the unit made in Step 10. This completes the banner top.

12. Lay the backing fabric (18″ × 40″) face-down on your work surface. Center the batting or fleece over the backing; then center the banner top face-up over the batting.

13. Pin-baste or baste the layers together. Machine- or hand-quilt along the seamlines, around each appliqué shape, and through the centers of the yellow strips, or in other quilting patterns of your choice.

14. Baste close inside the raw edges of the banner top, through all 3 layers of the banner. Trim away any excess batting and backing. Bind the edges of the banner with the black binding (see the General Directions chapter for binding information).

15. Cut the yellow ribbon into 3 equal lengths. Tie each into a small bow and tack one to the neck of each ghost, using yellow thread.

Autumn Leaves Table Runner and Potholders

Bring the colors of the outdoors inside this autumn. Finished size of runner: 16″ × 43″. Finished size of potholders: 7″ × 7″.

Materials Required*

- *½ yard natural-colored broadcloth*
- *½ yard brown print fabric for backings*
- *Various autumn-colored scrap fabrics, totalling ¾ yard (pieces should be at least 5″ × 5″)*
- *¾ yard craft fleece*
- *¾ yard fusible transfer webbing*
- *4 yards rust-colored ½″ extra-wide double-fold binding (unfolded width = 2″)*
- *All-purpose threads to match the fabrics*
- *8″ piece of ½″-wide rust-colored satin ribbon*

*Makes one runner and 2 potholders.

Directions

Note: All measurements, except for the appliqué pattern, include ¼″ seam allowances.

Table Runner

1. Trace 18 leaves (from Fig. 15–1) onto the paper side of fusible webbing, and cut them out. Fuse the webbing leaves to the fall-colored fabric scraps you choose, and cut them out of the fabric.

2. Cut one 16″ × 43″ rectangle from each of the following: the natural-colored fabric; the backing fabric; and the fleece. Fold the natural-colored rectangle in half lengthwise and press it to mark its centerline.

3. Mark the curves to be cut at the ends of the table runner onto the natural-colored rectangle by tracing out and enlarging the cutting guide (Fig. 15–2) onto paper; see the General Directions chapter for enlarging instructions. Then place the traced curve under the fabric and trace it onto the ends of the fabric rectangle (see photo and 15–3). Trace out the quilting line curves lightly from the enlarged Figure 15–2 onto the natural-colored cloth with light blue washable pencil. Join the quilting curves by tracing straight lines between them, parallel to the straight sides of the rectangle, with a yardstick.

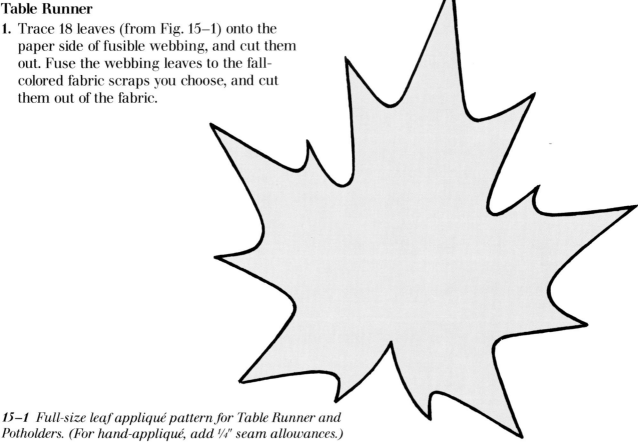

15–1 Full-size leaf appliqué pattern for Table Runner and Potholders. (For hand-appliqué, add ¼″ seam allowances.)

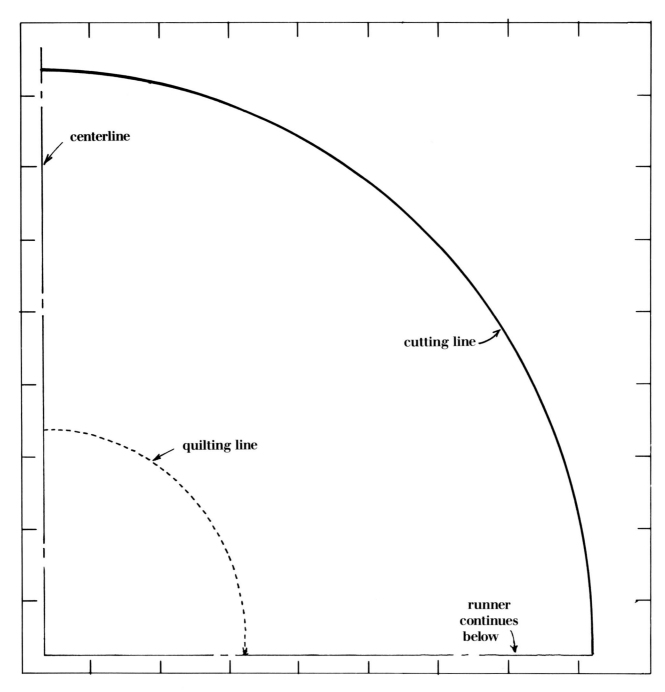

15–2 *Reduced cutting guide for the short ends of the runner. 1 box = 1″ × 1″.*

4. Trim away the excess fabric at the curves (see Fig. 15–3) to make the runner top.

5. Lightly trace 18 leaves with chalk or light blue washable pencil onto the runner top you cut in Step 4. Position one leaf at the center of each short end. Space 8 leaves evenly between the end ones on each long side. See the photo for placement of the leaves. The bottoms of the leaves should be ½″ in from the raw edges of the runner top. Fuse the leaves cut in Step 1 to the runner top.

6. Machine-appliqué each leaf in place with matching thread.

7. Place the backing rectangle you cut in Step 2 face-down on your work surface. Center the fleece rectangle over the backing. Center the runner top, face-up, over the fleece. Baste ½" in from the raw edge of the runner top through all 3 layers; then trim away the excess backing and fleece, using the runner top as a guide.

8. Pin or baste the rust-colored binding to the right side of the unit made in Step 7, with the raw edges of the binding and the runner aligned. Machine-stitch the binding to the unit with ¼" seam allowance. Turn over the rest of the binding and hand-stitch it to the runner back (see the General Directions chapter for more information on binding).

9. Quilt the runner by hand- or machine-stitching along the quilt lines you previously marked on the runner top. Stitch another line of quilting ¼" inside the first line of stitching.

Potholders

1. For each potholder, cut 7" × 7" squares of the following: natural-colored fabric; backing fabric; and craft fleece. Fold the fabric square in half and press it to mark the centerline.

2. Trace a leaf from Figure 15–1 onto the fusible webbing; then cut it out and fuse it to the scrap fabric. Cut out the leaf from the fabric and fuse it to the center of the natural-colored square (see photo).

3. Machine-appliqué the leaf in place with matching thread to make the potholder top.

4. Place the backing fabric square face-down on your work surface, center the batting square over it, and place the potholder top face-up over that. Pin-baste the three layers together ¼" in from the raw edge; trim any excess from the backing and binding.

5. Bind the potholder in the same way as the runner was bound (see Step 8, above).

6. Cut the ribbon into 2 equal lengths. Fold a length to form a loop, and tack the loop to the back of the potholder.

7. Repeat steps 1 through 6 to make the second potholder.

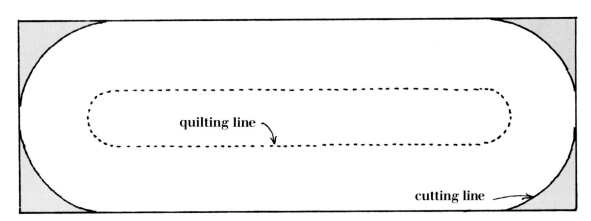

15–3 Diagram showing cutting and quilting lines for runner. Shaded areas are discarded.

Autumn Harvest Pillows

Stitch a bountiful autumn harvest this year. These pillows stitch up quickly and can be made from scraps you may already have in your sewing basket. Finished size of 16-patch pillow: 12″ × 12″. Finished size of pumpkin pillow: 14″ × 14″. Finished size of squash pillow: 16″ × 16″.

Materials Required for Set

- *½ yard unbleached muslin*
- *1 yard fabric for backings in a color you choose*
- *Scraps of fabrics in autumnal colors: including 7½″ square of orange for the pumpkin; a 5½″ × 9½″ piece of yellow fabric for the squash; and scraps of brown, green, mustard, and tan*
- *Sewing and quilting threads to match fabrics*
- *½ yard fusible transfer webbing*
- *Green embroidery floss*
- *White, yellow, and green piping*
- *12″ × 12″ pillow form*
- *14″ × 14″ pillow form*
- *16″ × 16″ pillow form*

Directions

Note: All measurements, except appliqué patterns, include ¼″ seam allowances. Piecing of patches and borders is done with right sides of material facing.

16-Patch Pillow

1. Cut 20 A squares, each 2½″ × 2½″, from scrap fabrics.

2. Stitch 4 A squares together to make a 4-block row (see Fig. 16–1, top).

3. Repeat Step 2 three more times for a total of 4 rows.

4. Stitch the 4 rows together to form the pieced pillow center, as shown in Figure 16–1.

5. To make the borders, cut 4 B strips, each 2½″ × 8½″, from muslin. Stitch one colored A square to each short end of two B strips (see Fig. 16–2, left and right). Set them aside.

6. Stitch the remaining two B strips to the top and bottom of the pillow center made in Step 4 (see Fig. 16–2).

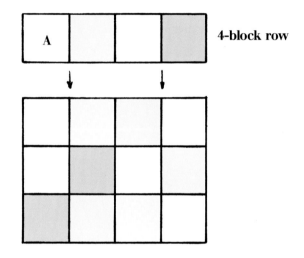

16–1 Stitch four rows together for the 16-Patch Pillow center.

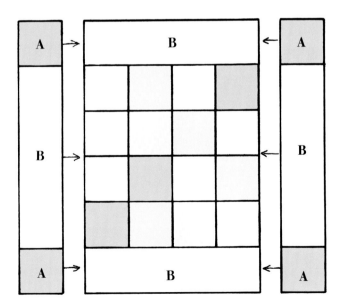

16–2 Attaching the borders on the 16-Patch Pillow top.

7. Stitch the pieced borders (A–B–A) made in Step 5 to the sides of the unit made in Step 6 (see Fig. 16–2). This completes the pillow top. Press.

8. Aligning the raw edges of the piping with those of the pillow top, baste a length of green piping approximately 50″ long around the edges of the pillow top on its right side (see the General Directions chapter for more piping information).

9. Cut a 12½″ square of fabric for the pillow's backing. Stitch the backing to the pillow top, with right sides together, along 3 sides. Clip the corners of the seam allowance to ease turning, but do not clip the seam. Turn the pillow cover right-side out and press it.

10. Insert the 12″ pillow form into the pillow cover, and stitch the opening closed to finish the pillow.

Pumpkin Pillow

1. Cut one 8½″ square from muslin. Fold the square in half and press it to mark its centerline. Center the square over the appliqué pattern (Fig. 16–3), and lightly trace the pattern onto the right side of the muslin with light blue washable pencil, including the embroidery pattern (dashed lines). Be sure the pattern doesn't extend into the ¼″ seam allowance around the square.

2. Trace the reversed appliqué pattern shapes from Figure 16–3 onto the back side of fusible webbing. (Trace the pumpkin as a whole shape. The front leaf will be fused over it.) Cut out the shapes from the webbing. Fuse the leaves to green fabric, the stem to brown fabric, and the pumpkin to orange fabric, all on the wrong sides of the fabric.

3. Cut out the shapes made in Step 2 from their respective fabrics, and fuse them in place on the muslin square. With light blue pencil, trace or draw the embroidery patterns that aren't already transferred to the leaves and pumpkin from Fig. 16–3.

4. Machine-appliqué the pieces to the muslin square, using threads that match the colors of the fabric. Machine satin-stitch down the center of the leaves with green thread. Embroider the tendrils by hand, using 2 strands of green embroidery floss, in stem stitch.

5. Refer to Figure 16–4 for steps 5 through 10. For the inner borders, cut 2 A strips, each 1½″ × 8½″, from a fabric you choose (mustard yellow in the model). Stitch the A strips to two opposite sides of the appliquéd muslin square.

6. Cut 2 B strips, each 1½″ × 10½″, from mustard yellow fabric or another color you choose, and stitch them to the top and bottom of the unit made in Step 5. Press.

7. Cut 4 C strips of a contrasting color of fabric (green in the model); each C strip is 2½″ × 10½″. Cut 4 D squares, each 2½″ × 2½″, from another color (rust in the model).

8. Stitch one C strip to the left side of the pillow center made in Step 6 and one to the right side.

9. Stitch one D square to each short end of the two remaining C strips. Sew these pieced borders to the top and bottom of the unit made in Step 8. This completes the pillow top.

10. Baste a length of yellow piping (approximately 60″ long) around the edges of the right side of the pillow top, with the raw edges of the piping and pillow top aligned.

11. Cut a 14½″ square of fabric for the backing.

12. Stitch the backing to the pillow top, with right sides together and ¼″ seam allowances, along 3 sides, leaving the bottom side open for turning. Clip the corners of the seam allowances to ease turning, but don't clip the seam.

13. Turn the pillow cover right-side out. Press. Insert the 14″ pillow form, and stitch the opening closed to complete the pillow.

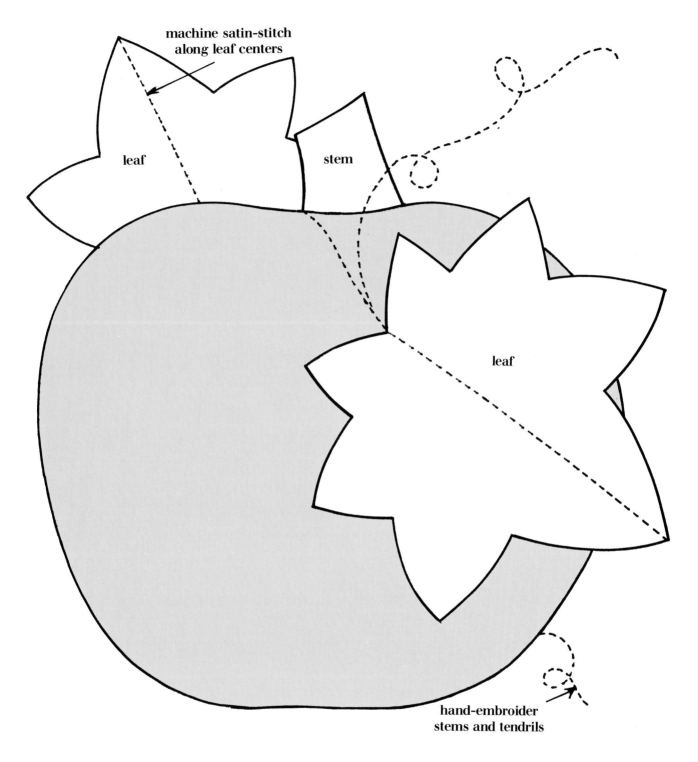

16–3 *Full-size appliqué pattern for Pumpkin Pillow. (If you will do hand-appliqué, add ¼" seam allowances around each piece.)*

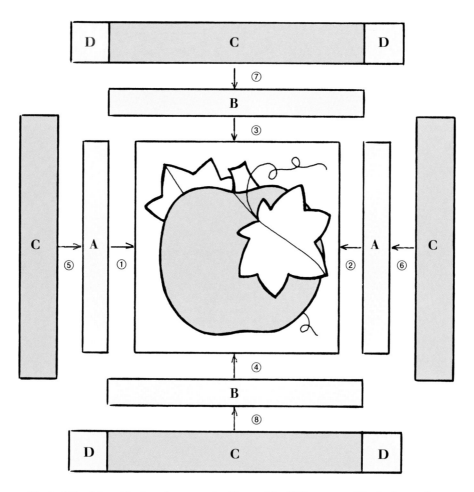

16–4 Attaching the borders on the Pumpkin Pillow top. Circled numbers indicate order of piecing.

Squash Pillow

1. Cut one 8½″ square from muslin. Fold it in half and press it to mark its centerline. Center the square over the appliqué pattern (Fig. 16–5), and lightly trace the pattern onto the right side of the muslin with light blue washable pencil, including the tendril embroidery patterns (dashed lines). Be sure the pattern doesn't extend into the ¼″ seam allowance.

2. Trace the reversed appliqué pattern shapes from Figure 16–5 onto the back side of fusible webbing. (Trace the squash as a whole shape. The front leaf will be fused over it.) Cut out the shapes from the webbing. Fuse the squash shape to yellow fabric; fuse the leaves to green fabrics.

3. Fuse the shapes made in Step 2 in place on the muslin square. Transfer any remaining embroidery marks from Figure 16–5 by laying the square with appliqué pieces over the full-size pattern.

4. Machine-appliqué the pieces in place, using threads that match the fabrics.

5. Machine satin-stitch down the centers of the leaves with green thread.

6. Hand-embroider the stems and tendrils, using 2 strands of green embroidery floss, in the stem stitch.

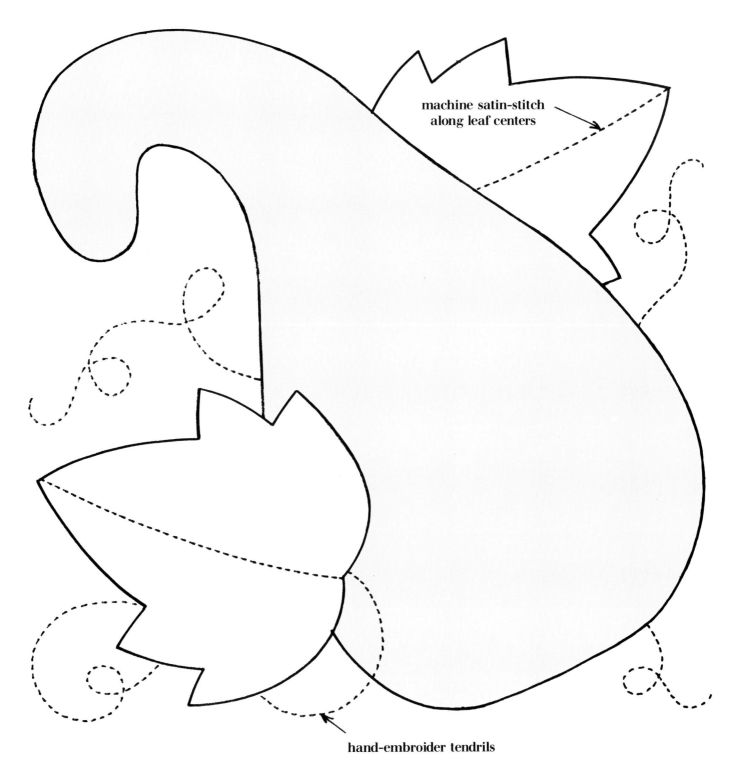

machine satin-stitch
along leaf centers

hand-embroider tendrils

16–5 *Full-size appliqué pattern for the Squash Pillow. (If you will do hand appliqué, add ¼" seam allowances around each piece.)*

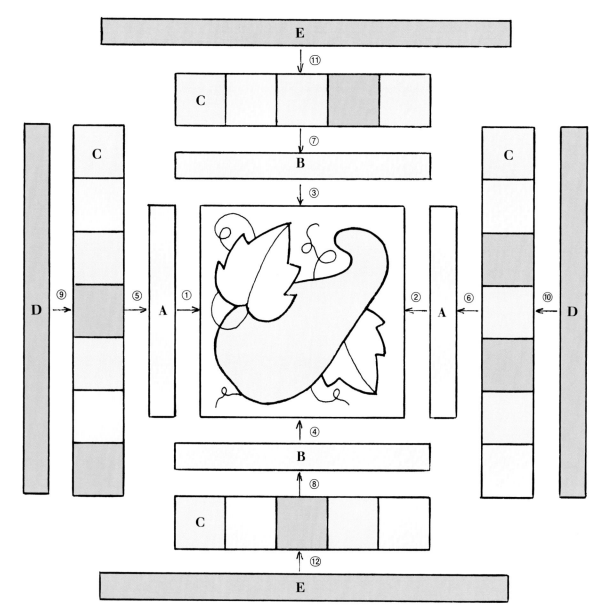

16–6 Construction diagram for the borders of the Squash Pillow. Circled numbers indicate the order of piecing the borders.

7. Refer to Figure 16–6 for steps 7 through 15. Cut 2 A strips (rust in the model), each 1½″ × 8½″, and stitch them to two opposite sides of the appliquéd muslin square.

8. Cut two B strips (rust in the model), each 1½″ × 10½″, and stitch them to the top and bottom of the unit made in Step 7. Set the unit aside for now.

9. To form the pieced borders, cut 24 C squares in various colors, each 2½″ × 2½″, from scrap yardage.

10. Stitch 5 C squares together in a row to form a short strip. Make another short strip the same way.

11. Stitch the short strips to the top and bottom of the pillow center made in Step 8. Set the unit aside.

12. Stitch 7 C squares together to form a long pieced strip. Make another long pieced strip the same way.

13. Attach the long pieced strips to the sides of the unit made in Step 11 (see Fig. 16–6, left and right). Press the unit.

14. Cut 2 D strips, each 1½″ × 14½″ (rust in the model, and stitch them to the sides of the unit made in Step 13.

15. Cut 2 E strips (rust in the model), each 1½″ × 16½″, and stitch them to the top and bottom of the unit made in Step 14. Press. This completes the pillow top.

16. Baste a length of white piping, approximately 66″ long, around the edges of the pillow top, with the raw edges of the pillow top and piping aligned (see the General Directions chapter for more information on piping).

17. Cut a 16½″ square of fabric for the pillow backing. Stitch the pillow front to the pillow backing, with right sides of fabric facing and ¼″ seam allowances, on three sides of the pillow, leaving the bottom edge open for turning. Clip the corners of the seam allowances for turning, but don't clip the seams. Turn the pillow cover right-side out and press it.

18. Insert the pillow form and stitch the opening closed to finish the pillow.

Wonderful Wintertime

Juggling Snowman Wall Hanging

Winter's a wonderful, magical time of year. If you don't have "real" snow, perhaps this sprightly snowman will do the trick instead! Finished size of banner: 21″ × 25″.

Materials Required

- *½ yard teal or teal print fabric (includes yardage for backing)*
- *½ yard white fabric*
- *⅓ yard each red print fabric and yellow print fabric*
- *Scraps of black fabric and pink fabric*
- *22″ × 26″ piece of fleece or quilt batting*
- *½ yard fusible transfer webbing*
- *Threads to match the fabrics*
- *Black embroidery floss*
- *5 black buttons, ¼″ wide or smaller*
- *3 yards yellow ½″ extra-wide double-folded bias binding (unfolded width = 2″)*

Directions

Note: All measurements, except appliqué patterns, include ¼″ seam allowance.

1. From the teal fabric, cut a 22″ × 26″ rectangle for the backing. Set it aside for now. From the remaining teal fabric cut: a rectangle 13½″ × 17½″, and 4 D strips, 21½″ × 2½″ each. Fold the 13½″ × 17½″ rectangle in quarters and press it to mark the center. Set the strips and the rectangles aside for now.

2. Trace out appliqué patterns 17–1a and 17–1b onto tracing paper, and join them at the arrow marks to make a whole pattern.

3. Trace the reversed snowman's body pattern onto the back of fusible webbing and cut it out of the webbing. Fuse the webbing snowman to white fabric and cut it out. Trace the embroidery and button markings onto the white fabric snowman. All tracing

on fabric should be done with washable, light blue pencil.

4. Trace the snowman's hat, cheeks, and scarf onto the back of fusible webbing and cut them out of the webbing. Fuse the hat to black fabric. Fuse the scarf to red print fabric. Fuse the cheeks to pink fabric. Cut out all the parts from the fabric.

5. Trace 5 stars from Figure 17–1b onto webbing, cut them out of the webbing, and fuse them to the back of the yellow print fabric. Then cut the stars out of the fabric.

6. Take the 13½″ × 17½″ teal rectangle cut in Step 1. Center the fabric snowman's body on the rectangle, with the bottom of the snowman's feet 1″ from the bottom of the rectangle (see color photo for reference). Fuse the snowman in place on the rectangle. Fuse the hat, cheeks, stars, and scarf in place also.

7. Machine-appliqué all the pieces in place, using threads that match the colors of the fabric pieces. Embroider the mouth by hand, using two strands of black embroidery floss, in the stem stitch (see hand-embroidery information in the General Directions chapter). Machine satin-stitch the hat and scarf details in red.

8. See Figure 17–2 for steps 8–13. Cut 2 A strips, 2½″ × 17½″ each, from red print fabric. Stitch them to the long sides of the appliquéd teal rectangle.

9. Cut 2 B strips, each 2½″ × 13½″, from the red print fabric.

10. Cut 4 C squares, 2½″ × 2½″ each, from the yellow print fabric.

11. Attach a yellow C square to the short ends of each B strip.

12. Attach one of the pieced strips made in Step 11 to the top of the unit made in Step 8, and another of the pieced strips to the bottom of the unit (see Fig. 17–2).

13. Take two of the teal D strips (21½″ × 2½″, cut in Step 1), and stitch one to each long

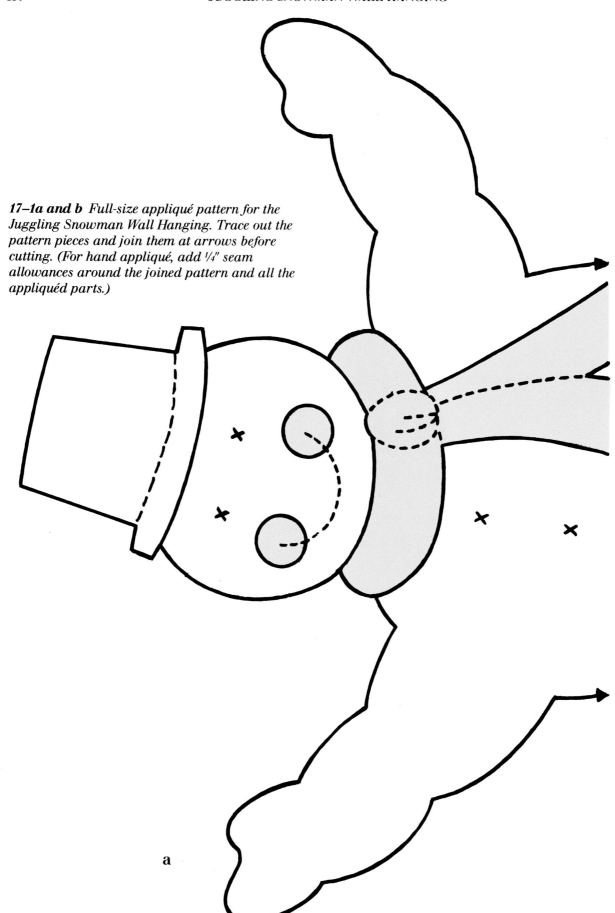

17–1a and b *Full-size appliqué pattern for the Juggling Snowman Wall Hanging. Trace out the pattern pieces and join them at arrows before cutting. (For hand appliqué, add ¼″ seam allowances around the joined pattern and all the appliquéd parts.)*

a

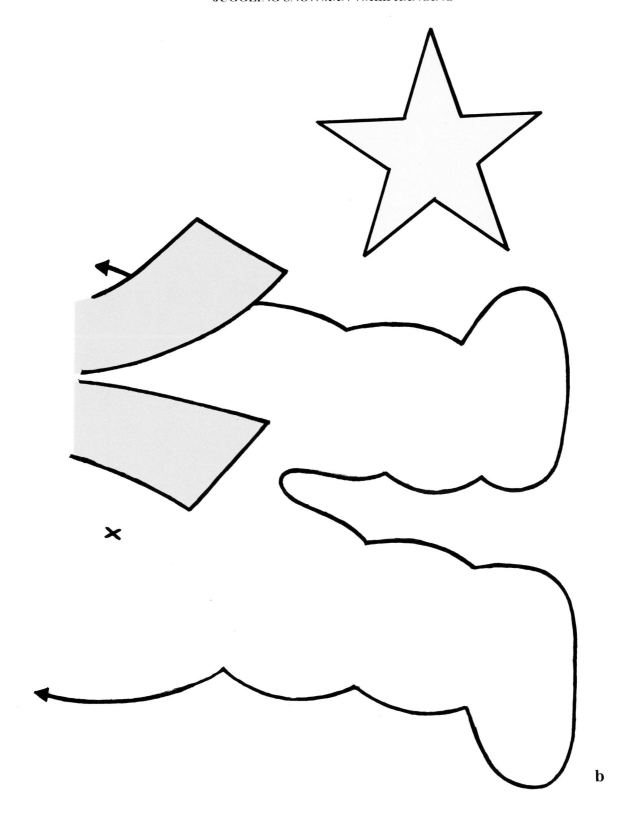

x

b

side of the unit made in Step 12 (see Fig. 17–2).

14. Take the remaining teal D strips, which are 21½″ × 2½″ (cut in Step 1), and attach one to the top and one to the bottom of the unit made in Step 13 (see Fig. 17–2). This completes the wall hanging top. Press it.

15. Lay the precut backing piece (made in Step 1) face-down on your work surface. Center the fleece or batting over the backing. Center the wall hanging, face-up, over the fleece.

16. Pin-baste or baste the three layers together. Machine-quilt ¼″ from the seamlines, or in

some other pattern you like. Then baste ½″ in from the edges of the wall hanging top. Trim away the excess batting and backing.

17. Take the yellow bias binding and baste one edge of it to the quilt top, with raw edges aligned. Stitch it to the quilt all around; remove the basting; turn the unattached side of the binding to the back of the quilt, and hand-stitch it in place (see the General Directions chapter for more information on binding).

18. Stitch the black buttons on the snowman with black thread; each button is indicated on the pattern by a small x.

Hannukah Wall Hanging

The menorah (eight-branched candelabrum) and dreidel (top) are symbols of the Jewish holiday of Hannukah. The wall hanging is done in traditional colors. Finished size of banner: 30″ × 33″.

Materials Required

- *⅔ yard light blue fabric*

- *½ yard each of white fabric and light yellow fabric*

- *¼ yard deep yellow fabric*

- *1 yard apricot (light orange) fabric (includes yardage for backing)*

- *1 yard fusible transfer webbing*

- *33″ × 36″ piece of batting or fleece*

- *½ yard ¼″-wide light blue satin ribbon*

- *10″ scrap of ¼″-wide apricot (light orange) satin ribbon*

- *Machine embroidery threads to match fabrics*

- *All-purpose threads in white and yellow*

- *4 yards of yellow ½″ extra-wide double-fold bias binding (unfolded width = 2″)*

Directions

Note: All measurements, except appliqué patterns, include ¼″ seam allowances.

1. Cut a 20½″ × 23½″ rectangle from blue fabric for the center part. Fold it in half lengthwise and press it to mark the centerline. Cut a 33″ × 36″ rectangle from apricot fabric for the backing. Set both rectangles aside.

2. From white fabric, cut 2 A strips, 5½″ × 23½″ each, for side borders. For the top and bottom borders, cut 2 B strips, 5½″ × 20½″ each, from white fabric (see Fig. 18–1).

3. Cut 4 C squares, 5½″ × 5½″ each, from light yellow fabric for the corners.

4. Fold the 4 white borders in half crosswise and press them to mark the centers for

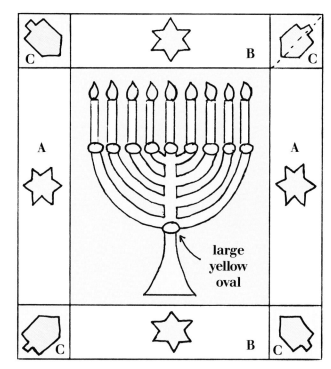

18–1 Construction diagram for the Hannukah Wall Hanging.

appliqué positioning. Fold each corner square in half on the diagonal and press it to mark an appliqué placement line.

5. Enlarge the menorah top half-pattern in Figure 18–2, flip it over, and retrace it on another piece of tracing paper for the right side of the menorah top (see the General Directions chapter for help in enlarging a pattern). Join the two pattern parts, and then trace the menorah top onto the paper side of fusible webbing and cut it out.

6. Trace the following from Figure 18–3 onto the fusible webbing, and cut them out of the webbing; one menorah bottom, 9 flames, 9 candles, 4 dreidels, one large oval, 9 small ovals, and 4 stars.

7. Fuse the webbing pieces to the wrong sides of following fabrics, and then cut them out:
   menorah top and bottom: light yellow
   flames and dreidels: apricot
   stars: blue
   candles: white
   large and small ovals: dark yellow

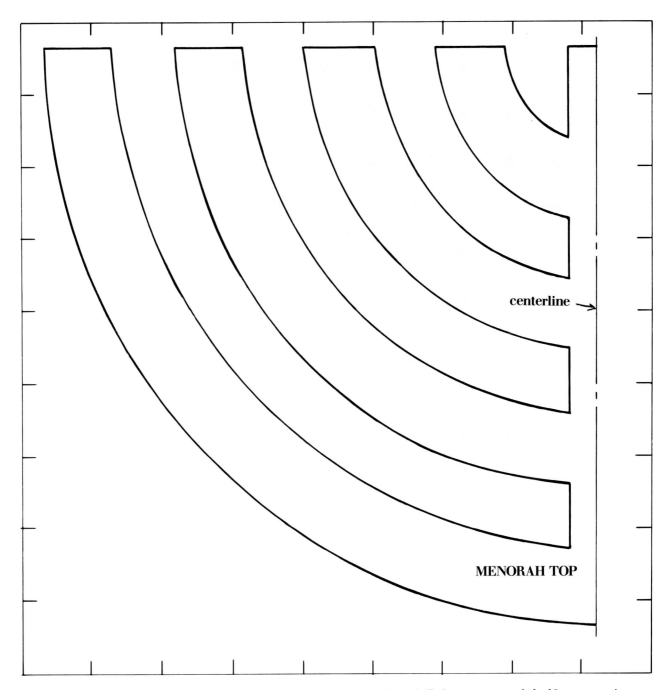

centerline →

MENORAH TOP

18-2 Reduced appliqué pattern for menorah top. 1 box = 1" × 1". Enlarge menorah half-pattern given here, reverse it and trace again, and join the two halves of the pattern on the centerline. (For hand appliqué, add ¼" seam allowances around enlarged pattern.)

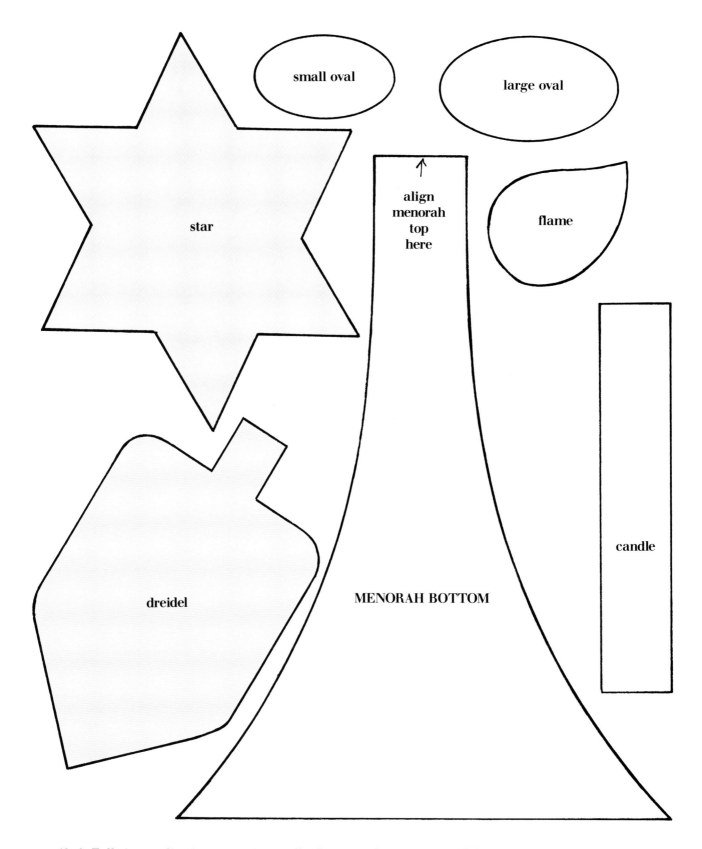

18–3 *Full-size appliqué patterns for candle, flame, ovals, star, menorah bottom, and dreidel. (For hand appliqué, add ¼″ seam allowances around the patterns.)*

8. Fuse the fabric menorah to the blue rectangle cut in Step 1, with the bottom of the menorah 1½″ from the raw edge of the bottom of the blue rectangle, and the centerline of the menorah over the center fold of the rectangle. The top of the menorah should be centered over the bottom of the menorah and sit directly above it. Fuse a candle directly above each candleholder (see Fig. 18–4) and then fuse one small yellow oval over the place where the candle meets the candleholder, covering the raw edges of both the candleholder and the candle. Fuse a flame to the top of each candle.

9. Fuse the large yellow oval to the central stem of the menorah (see Fig. 18–1), covering the raw edges of the two pieces below.

10. Fuse one star to the center of each white border strip (see Fig. 18–1). Fuse one dreidel to each light yellow corner block, with the dreidel's central line on the square's diagonal (see Fig. 18–1).

11. Machine appliqué each piece in place, using shades of machine embroidery thread that match each fabric.

12. See Figure 18–1 for border positions. Border piecing is done with right sides of material facing and ¼″ seam allowances. Using white all-purpose thread, stitch the side borders (A), cut in Step 2, to the central, appliquéd blue rectangle. Set it aside.

13. Stitch one yellow C block, aligned as in Figure 18–1, to each short end of the B strips cut in Step 2. They will be the top and bottom borders. Stitch them to the top and bottom of the wall hanging. Press the seams towards the outer edges.

14. Lay the precut backing fabric face-down on your work surface. Center the fleece over the backing and quilt the wall hanging in a design that is pleasing to you. After quilting,

baste the wall hanging about ¼″ in from the quilt top edges. Trim off any excess batting or backing.

15. Pin the yellow bias binding, with raw edges of the binding and the quilt top edges aligned, to the top layer of the quilt. Sew it to the quilt with yellow all-purpose thread and ¼″ seam allowance. Turn over the loose edge of the binding to the back of the quilt and stitch it in place. (See the General Directions chapter for further binding information.)

16. Cut the blue ribbon into 4 equal lengths and tie each piece into a small bow. Tack one bow to each dreidel top (see photo). Tie the length of apricot ribbon into a bow and tack it in place on the menorah, just below the large oval.

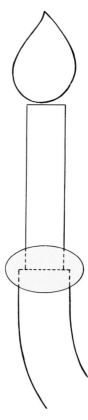

18–4 Fuse each candle directly over its candleholder. Fuse a small yellow oval in place over the raw ends of both.

Christmas Breakfast Table Settings

Make these settings for those busy Christmas mornings. Finished size of place mat: 17″ × 13″. Finished napkin size: 18″ × 18″. The materials include enough fabric for two napkins and two place mats.

Materials Required for Two Settings

- *1 yard green print fabric*
- *½ yard red print fabric with a border stripe*
- *¼ yard white fabric*
- *¼ yard red print fabric (for triangles)*
- *4 yards of white piping*
- *2 pieces of craft fleece, each 14″ × 18″*
- *All-purpose threads to match the fabrics*

Directions

Note: All measurements include ¼″ seam allowances. Piecing is done with right sides of material facing, unless otherwise noted.

To Make Two Mats and Two Napkins

1. From the green print fabric, cut two pieces, each 14″ × 18″, for place mat backings, and cut two 18½″ squares for napkins. Turn under a ¼″ hem around all 4 sides of each napkin square (not on the place mats, however), and stitch it down with matching thread. Press the napkins. Set the backings and napkins aside.

2. From the remaining green fabric cut 24 squares, using the square template in Figure 19–1.

3. Using the triangle template in Figure 19–1, cut 24 white triangles and 24 red print triangles (the latter are from the ¼″ yard of red print fabric). Stitch one red triangle to one white triangle on their long sides, and repeat this to make 24 pieced squares (12 for each place mat).

4. Alternate pieced squares with green squares and sew together a row of six squares (see 19–2a, top). Follow Figure 19–2a to make 4 rows for each place mat (a total of 8 rows) in the same manner.

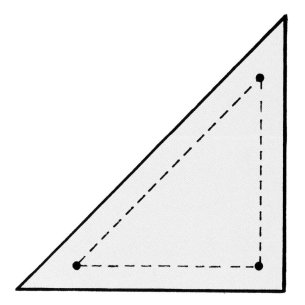

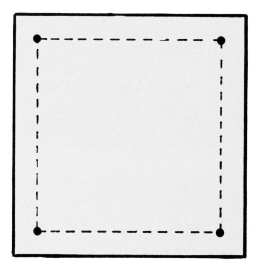

19–1 Templates for triangle and square pieces of the Christmas Breakfast Table Settings. The solid line is the cutting line; the dashed line is the stitching line.

5. For each place mat, stitch 4 rows together, as shown in Figure 19–2b.

6. To make the top and bottom borders, cut 4 strips (2 for each place mat), each 3″ × 17½″, from the red fabric with the center stripe. Fold each one in half crosswise and press them to mark their centers. Center the strips on the top and bottom edges of each place mat. With red thread and ¼″ seam allowance, stitch the strips to the top and bottom of each mat, starting and stopping ¼″ from the corner of the place mat, having right sides of fabrics facing (Fig. 19–3a). Don't trim the excess at the ends of the strips.

7. For the side borders, cut four 3″ × 14½″ strips (2 for each place mat) from the red stripe fabric. Center them, as you did for the previous borders, and stitch two to each place mat center (Fig. 19–3b), stopping ¼″ from the corner of the pieced center (see dots in Fig. 19–3b). Mitre the corners by aligning the short ends of the two borders that meet at each corner and stitching them together, with right sides of material facing, at a 45° angle to the stitching that attached the border (see Fig. 19–3c). Trim away the excess fabric from the mitres. Press the borders open to show the finished mitre (see Fig. 19–3d). Repeat this step for all 4 corners to complete each place mat top.

8. Baste piping around the edges on the right side of each place mat, with raw edges of the mat and piping even, using a ¼″ seam allowance. Baste a fleece rectangle to the back side of each place mat top, along the raw edges. Trim away any excess fleece.

9. Put each place mat top and back together, with right sides facing, and stitch them together around the edges, with ¼″ seam allowances; leave a 3″ opening along one edge for turning. Clip the corners of the seam allowances to ease turning, and turn the mats right-side out. Press the place mats. Stitch the 3″ openings closed.

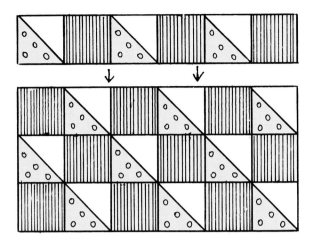

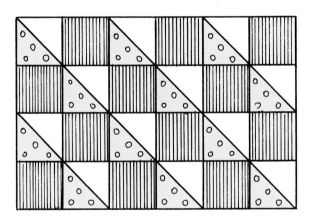

19–2 Top: *a pieced, 6-square row is joined.* Bottom: *4 rows stitched together to form the place mat center. Key:*

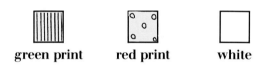

green print   red print   white

10. Pin or baste the center areas of the place mats to avoid shifting of the layers. Quilt along the border seamlines and diagonally inside each place mat to complete them.

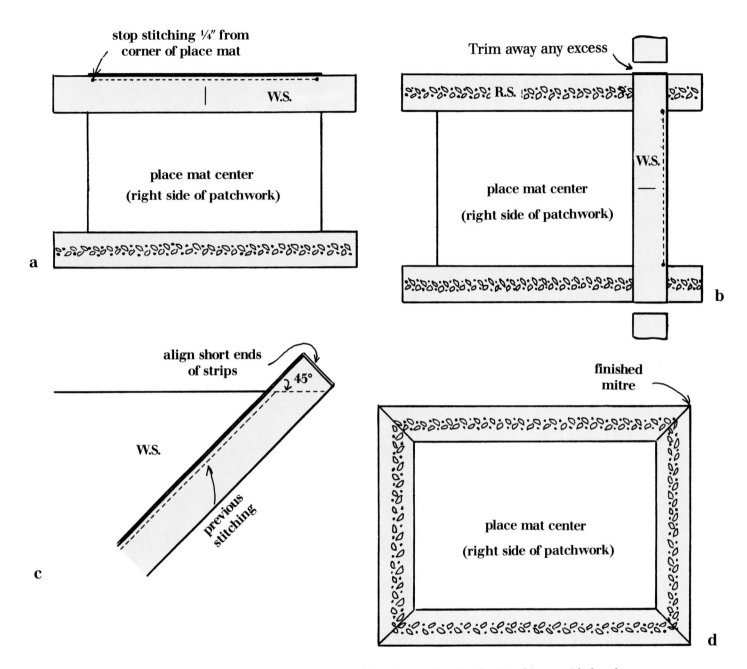

19–3 *Mitring corners of a place mat.* **a:** *Attaching the top border.* **b:** *Attaching a side border.* **c:** *Stitching the borders at a 45° angle.* **d:** *Finished place mat top. Dashed lines are sewing lines. See text for details.*

Christmas Tree Skirt and Stocking

A lively duo for your holiday decorating! Finished size of tree skirt: 50″ in diameter, including ruffle. Finished size of stocking: approximately 8½″ × 15″.

Materials Required

For tree skirt

- *1½ yards white broadcloth*
- *1½ yards green print fabric for the backing*
- *2 yards red print fabric*
- *½ yard solid green fabric*
- *45" square of craft fleece or quilt batting*
- *3 yards 1"-wide red satin ribbon*
- *3 yards ½"-wide green satin ribbon*
- *½ yard fusible transfer webbing*
- *4 yards of green piping*
- *Pencil*
- *28" of string*
- *Safety pin*

For *each* stocking

- *2 pieces of white broadcloth, 12" × 18" each*
- *2 pieces of craft fleece, 12" × 18" each*
- *2 pieces of green print fabric for the lining, 12" × 18" each*
- *6" × 28" strip of red printed fabric for the ruffle*
- *6" square of red print fabric*
- *5" square of solid green fabric*
- *5" square of fusible webbing*
- *12" piece of ½"-wide red satin ribbon*
- *14" piece of ½" extra-wide double-fold green bias binding (unfolded width = 2")*

Directions

Note: All measurements, except appliqué patterns, include ¼" seam allowances.

Tree Skirt

1. Fold the 1½" yards of white broadcloth into quarters. Cut one 44"-diameter circle from the white broadcloth, as shown in Figure 20–1.

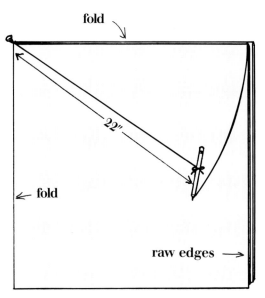

20–1 Cutting a 44"-diameter circle for the tree skirt. Fold the cloth in quarters. Pin the fabric through all layers so it doesn't move. Tack one end of a string at the center of the two folds. Tie a pencil at the other end so that the distance between the pencil point and the pin (the radius) is 22". Swing a curve around the quarter to mark the fabric; then cut out the circle on the curve and open it out.

2. Open out the circle. Referring to Figure 20–2, draw a 22"-diameter (11"-radius) circle in the center of the white cloth circle. Draw a 6"-diameter (3"-radius) circle in the center of the 22" circle. Mark the quarter-fold lines, shown by the dotted lines on Figure 20–2. Draw another set of lines at the halfway points between the quarter-fold lines.

3. Carefully cut out the center 6" circle. Along one fold line, mark a 6" side opening, and mark a wedge from the outer edge to the center of the circle (see Fig. 20-2). Do not cut the wedge out yet.

4. Using the large white cloth circle as a pattern, cut a 44"-diameter circle from both the green print fabric (for the backing) and the fleece. Cut a 6"-diameter central hole in the backing and batting, using the white cloth circle as a pattern. Set them aside.

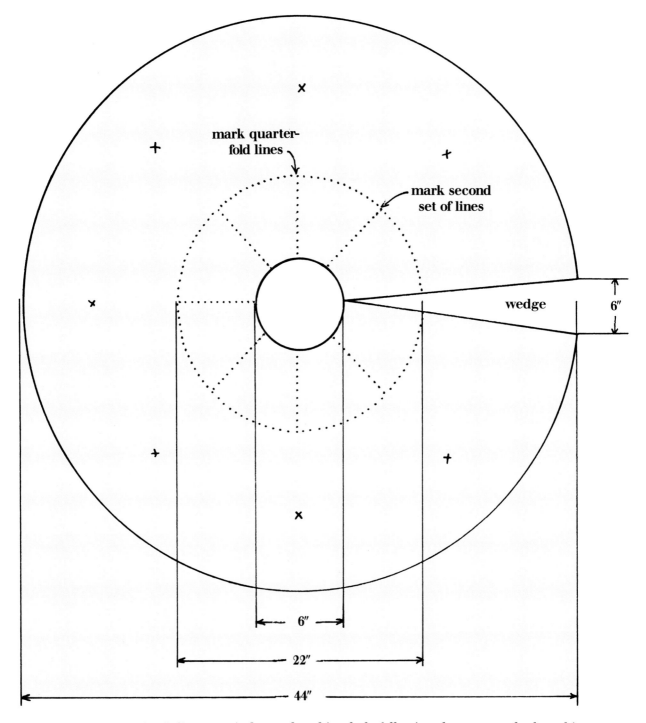

20–2 *Draw 6"- and 22"-diameter circles on the white cloth, following the same method used in Fig. 20–1. Mark the quarter and eighth lines (dotted lines) and the wedge.*

20–3 Full-size appliqué pattern for the tree skirt (large wreath). (If you will do hand appliqué, add ¼″ seam allowances.)

5. Trace 7 large wreaths (Fig. 20–3) onto the fusible webbing, and cut them out of the webbing. Fuse the webbing wreaths to the solid green fabric and cut out the wreaths. Fuse the fabric wreaths to the white cloth circle, in the places indicated by an × on Figure 20–2; machine-appliqué them in place.

6. Cut seven 8¼″ pieces of ½″-wide green ribbon, and appliqué them to the marked, spokelike lines between the middle circle and the cut-out center of the white fabric circle (see Fig. 20–2).

7. Cut one 1″ × 72″ strip on the bias from the red print fabric. Fold and press under ¼″ along each long edge. Appliqué the bias strip along the line marking the 22″-diameter circle, covering the raw edges of the green ribbon "spokes" as you come to them.

8. Cut out the wedge you marked in Step 3.

9. Baste green piping to the outer edge of the white circle, with raw edges aligned. (See the General Directions chapter for more information on piping, if necessary.)

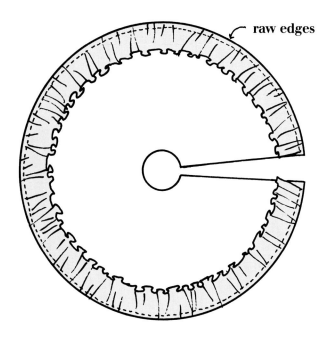

raw edges

20–4 Basting the ruffle to the tree skirt.

10. For the ruffle, cut seven 6½″ × 44½″ strips from the red print fabric. Stitch the strips together along their short ends to make one long strip. Fold the strip in half, with right sides of the fabric together, down the length of the strip. Stitch the piece across the short ends to close them. Turn the strip right-side out. Align the raw edges down the entire length of the strip and press it. Gather the strip along the raw edges with two lines of basting stitches in the seam allowance. Baste the ruffle to the outer edge of the right side of the white circle, distributing the fullness evenly (Fig. 20–4). The raw edges of the ruffle should align with the raw edge of the circle and piping.

11. Baste the fleece circle cut in Step 4 to the wrong side of the white appliquéd circle.

12. Stitch the white appliquéd tree skirt top (with its attached fleece, ruffle, and piping) to the backing, with right sides together and ¼″ seam allowances, along the outer edge and at the sides of the wedge, and around the small circle at the center, leaving a 6″ opening along one wedge side for turning the unit right-side out. Clip the seam allowances to ease turning. Turn the unit

right-side out through the opening. Stitch the turning opening closed.

13. Cut two 12″ pieces of the remaining green ribbon. Tack one piece to each side of the 6″-diameter center circle. You will be able to tie the ribbons into a bow to secure the skirt around the tree with them later.

14. Cut the red ribbon into 7 equal lengths. Tie each into a 5″-wide bow. Tack one bow to each wreath (see photo).

Stocking

1. Trace out the full stocking pattern from figures 20–6a and 20–6b onto a large piece of paper, aligning the register marks (heavy arrows) of the pattern parts to form one unit.

2. Trace and cut the stocking pattern from both 12″ × 18″ white cloth rectangles.

3. Trace one small wreath (Fig. 20–5) and one heel and toe piece (see Fig. 20–6a) onto fusible webbing, and cut them out of the webbing. Fuse the webbing wreath to the back of the solid green fabric, and fuse the heel and toe webbing pieces to the back of the 6″ red print fabric square. Cut out the shapes from the fabrics and appliqué them in place on the stocking front (see photo for wreath position).

4. Using the stocking pattern, cut a stocking shape from each piece of fleece, and baste one to the wrong side of each white stocking piece.

5. From the pattern, trace and cut two stocking shapes from the green print fabric lining pieces. Set them aside.

6. Stitch the two white-cloth-plus-fleece stocking pieces together, with right sides of the white cloth facing, leaving the top edge open, to make the outer stocking. Clip the curves of the seam allowances and turn the outer stocking right-side out. Set the unit aside.

7. Stitch together the two green lining stocking shapes, with right sides together,

20–5 Full-size appliqué pattern for stocking (small wreath). (If you will do hand appliqué, add ¼″ seam allowances.)

leaving the top edge open. Do not turn the unit right-side out.

8. Insert the lining stocking into the outer stocking made in Step 6, aligning the seamlines. Baste the lining to the outer stocking along the top edge.

9. For the stocking ruffle, fold the 6″ × 28″ red strip in half along its length, with its right sides facing in. Stitch across the short ends of the strip to close them. Turn the strip right-side out. Fold it in half across its length, to make a 4-thickness piece. Align all the raw edges and baste through all 4 thicknesses in the seam allowance.

10. Gather the raw edges of the ruffle to fit the stocking opening, and baste the ruffle to the outside of the stocking, aligning the stocking's and ruffle's raw edges.

11. Bind the top of the stocking with green bias binding: align the binding's raw edge with the ruffle's raw edges on the outside of the stocking. Sew the binding around the outside edge. Turn the long raw edge of the binding to the inside, and slipstitch it in place (see the General Directions chapter for more information on binding, if necessary).

12. Cut a 4″ piece of the red ribbon. Fold the piece in half to form a loop. Tack the loop to the inside of the stocking, just below the binding, to make a hanging loop. Tie the remaining ribbon into a bow and tack it in place on the wreath.

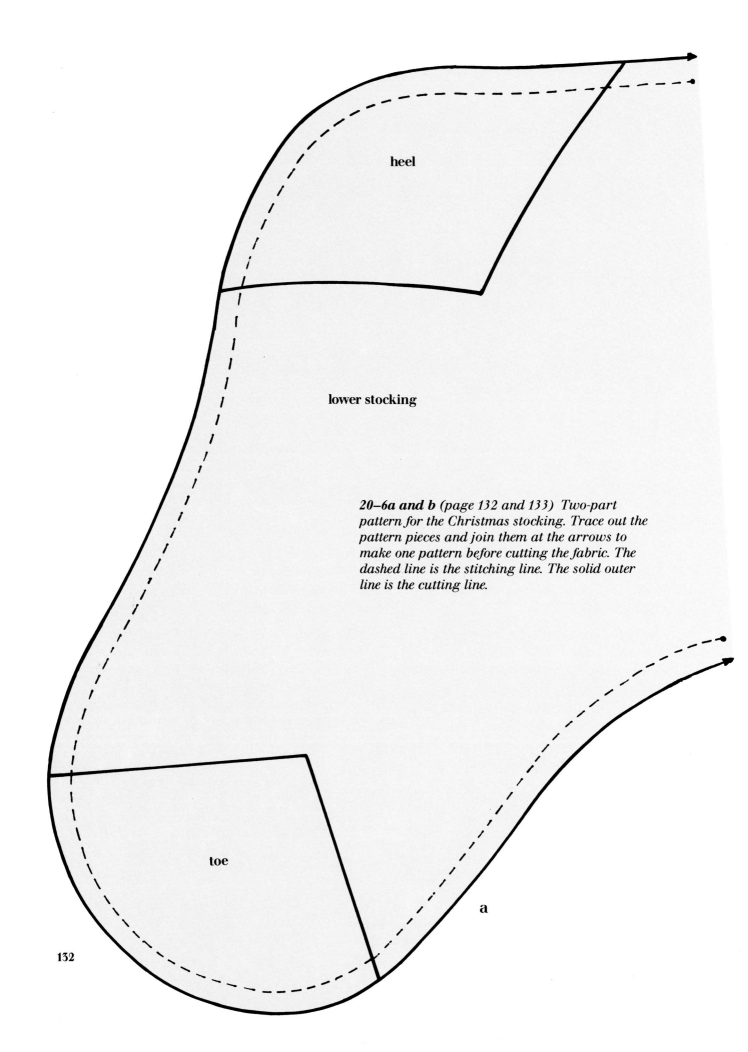

heel

lower stocking

20–6a and b (page 132 and 133) Two-part pattern for the Christmas stocking. Trace out the pattern pieces and join them at the arrows to make one pattern before cutting the fabric. The dashed line is the stitching line. The solid outer line is the cutting line.

toe

a

upper stocking

b

Snowflake Christmas Throw Pillows

Tuck a snowflake pillow into your coziest chair, brew a nice hot cup of tea, and enjoy the season. Finished pillow size: 14″ × 14″.

Materials for Two Pillows

- *1 yard red print fabric*
- *1 yard green print fabric*
- *½ yard white fabric*
- *Threads to match fabrics*
- *White rayon machine embroidery thread (optional)*
- *2 pillow forms, 14″ × 14″ each*
- *4 yards of white piping*
- *2 squares fusible transfer webbing, 9″ × 9″ each*

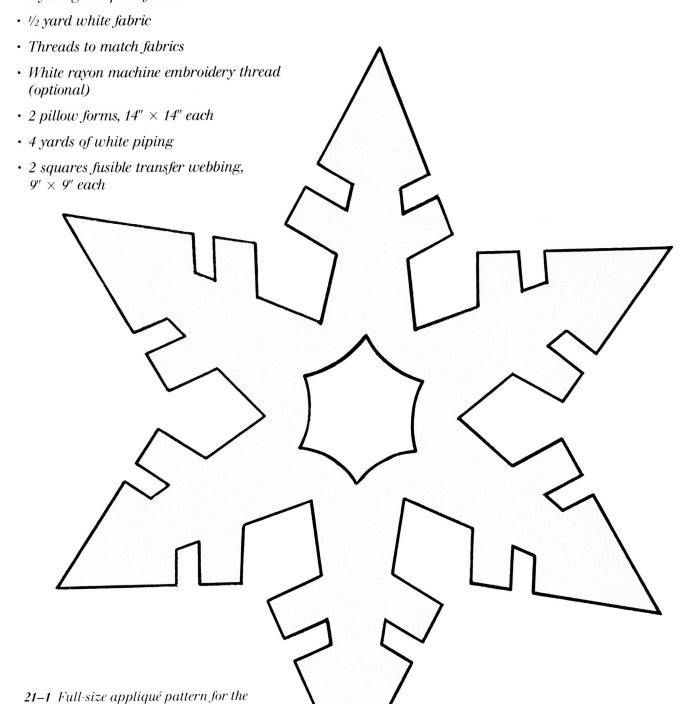

21–1 *Full-size appliqué pattern for the Snowflake Christmas Throw Pillows. If you will do hand appliqué, add ¼″ seam allowances. Cut one snowflake for each pillow.*

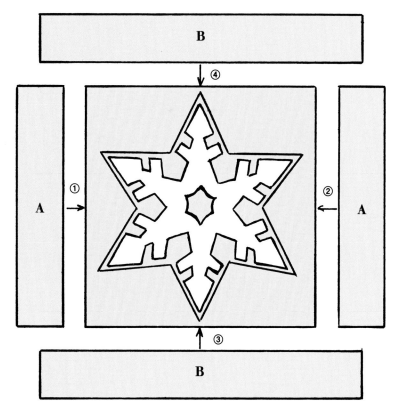

21–2 Attaching the border strips to the snowflake square. Circled numbers indicate the order of piecing.

Directions

Note: All measurements, except appliqué patterns, include ¼″ seam allowances.

**To Make Two Pillows
(One Red, One Green)**

1. Cut a 10½″ square from red print fabric and one from green print fabric. Fold each square in quarters and press it to mark the center.

2. Trace one snowflake (Fig. 21–1) onto each piece of fusible webbing, cut them out, and fuse the webbing snowflakes to the wrong side of the white fabric.

3. Cut out the snowflakes and fuse one to the center of the red print square and one to the center of the green print square (see photo).

4. With white thread, appliqué the snowflakes in place; then stitch an outline of medium-width (⅛″) white machine satin stitch around each snowflake, ¼″ outside the appliquéd snowflakes' edges (see photo). Set the squares aside.

5. Cut the following from *both* the red and green print fabric: two A strips, 2½″ × 10½″ each; two B strips, 2½″ × 14½″ each. The green strips are the borders for the red appliquéd square; the red strips are the borders for the green appliquéd square (see photo).

6. With right sides of material facing and ¼″ seam allowances, stitch the A strips to two opposite sides of each snowflake square. Press. Stitch the B strips to the remaining sides of the square, with right sides facing and ¼″ seam allowances (Fig. 21–2). Repeat this for the second snowflake square. This completes the pillow tops.

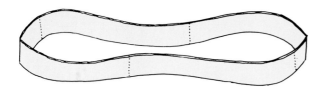

21–3 Making a ruffle. With pencil lines, divide the strip into 4 equal parts.

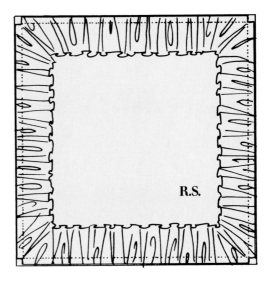

21–4 Distributing the ruffle. Place the marked parts at the corners of the pillow top, and distribute the fullness between the marks. Baste the ruffle to the right side of the pillow top, with raw edges aligned.

7. Baste the white piping around the edges of each pillow top on the right side of the fabric, with raw edges aligned and ¼" seam allowance. (See the General Directions chapter for further information about piping.) Cut a 14½" square of red print fabric for the red pillow back and a 14½" square of green print fabric for the green pillow back. Set them aside for now.

8. For the red pillow ruffle, cut three 44" × 7" strips from the red print fabric. Stitch the strips together by their short ends to make a long band. Fold the band in half lengthwise with the right side of material facing in, aligning raw edges to make a 44" × 3½" rectangle. Pin the two layers of each short end together and stitch across each end with a ¼" seam allowance to hem the end. Turn the ruffle right-side out and press it.

9. With pencil or chalk marks, divide the length of the band into 4 equal sections (Fig. 21–3). Make a ¼" cut into the seam allowance at each mark. Gather the folded ruffle on its raw edges between each cut with basting. Place the ruffle's cut marks at the corners of the pillow top made in Step 7, adjusting the ruffle's fullness evenly between the cut marks. Baste the ruffle to the right side of the pillow top, with raw edges aligned (Fig. 21–4).

10. Take the 14½" red print square pillow backing. Stitch the red pillow top to the red pillow backing, with right sides together, along 3 sides, leaving the bottom open for turning. Clip the seam allowance at the corners to ease turning, and turn the pillow cover right-side out. Insert the pillow form in the cover, and stitch the opening closed.

11. For the green pillow, repeat steps 8–10 with green print fabric, the green print square, and the green appliquéd pillow top.

Holiday Apron and Potholder

Any hostess would enjoy wearing one of these aprons for a special gathering, or perhaps receiving one of these sets as a gift. Apron size: 31″ × 36″. Potholder size: 10″ × 10″.

Materials Required for Set

- *½ yard white fabric*
- *2 yards green print fabric*
- *1 yard red print fabric*
- *Scraps of yellow fabric*
- *½ yard fusible transfer webbing*
- *6″ piece of ¼″-wide yellow satin ribbon*
- *Threads to match fabrics*
- *2 pieces of craft fleece, 10″ × 10″ each*

Directions

Note: Except for appliqué patterns, ¼″ seam allowances are included in the given measurements. Construction is done with right sides of fabric facing.

Potholder

1. Cut a 6½″ square of white fabric, fold it in half, and press it to mark the center.

2. Cut 2 strips of green fabric, 2½″ × 6½″ each, and stitch them to two opposite sides of the white square with right sides of fabric facing. Press the seams open. Cut 2 strips of green fabric, 2½″ × 10½″ each, and stitch them to the remaining 2 sides of the unit, with right sides of fabric facing. Press.

3. From Figure 22–1, trace one flower, one flower center, and 4 leaves onto fusible webbing, and cut them out of the webbing.

4. Fuse the flower center to yellow fabric; fuse the flower to red print fabric; fuse the leaves to green print fabric; and cut them all out. All are fused on the wrong sides of the fabrics.

5. With the photo for reference, center the flower on the square's center, and fuse the flower and its center to the white square, with one leaf extended into each corner. Machine appliqué the pieces in place with thread that matches each fabric.

6. Cut a 10½″ square of green fabric for the potholder backing. Pin the backing and potholder front together, with right sides facing. Fold the piece of yellow ribbon in half to make a loop. Insert the ribbon, with the loop facing in, into the seam area between the front and backing pieces, with the ribbon's raw ends extending beyond the corner. Stitch the potholder front and backing together, leaving a 4″ opening along one side for turning. Clip the corners of the seam allowance. Turn the unit right-side out.

7. Take the 10″ × 10″ pieces of fleece and insert them as a double layer in the unit you made in Step 6. Stitch the opening closed. Machine-quilt the unit along the outer edges of the white square.

Apron

Overview: The apron skirt and bib are made as 2 separate units and then joined.

1. For the appliquéd band in the apron skirt, cut one strip of white fabric, 6½″ × 31″.

2. From Figure 22–1, trace 2 swags, 3 flowers, and 3 flower centers onto the back of fusible webbing and cut them out of the webbing.

3. Fuse the swags to green print fabric, the flower centers to yellow fabric, and the flowers to the red print fabric. (All are fused on the wrong side of the fabrics.) Cut out the shapes.

4. Arrange the shapes on the white strip cut in Step 1, starting with the center flower and working out to the sides. On the right side of the fabric, lightly trace around the shapes with chalk or light blue washable pencil to mark their positions. Then fuse and appliqué the pieces in place with matching threads.

22–1 Full-size appliqué patterns for the Holiday Apron and Potholder. If you will do hand appliqué, add ¼″ seam allowances around each piece.

5. For the red print bands, cut 2 strips, 2″ × 31″ each. Stitch one red band to each long edge of the white appliquéd band (see Fig. 22–2). Press.

6. Cut a 2½″ × 31″ strip from green print fabric and stitch it to the bottom of the unit made in Step 5 (see photo and Fig. 22–2).

7. Cut a 14½″ × 31″ strip of green print fabric, and stitch it above the unit made in Step 6.

8. Finish the raw edges of the apron skirt with zigzag stitch along the apron sides and bottom; then turn under ¼″ to the back side of the apron, and stitch it down to hem the 3 sides. Press.

9. Gather the upper edge of the apron skirt with 2 rows of basting stitches in the seam allowance. Set it aside for now.

10. To make the upper apron (bib), cut out and appliqué one square and add borders as you did for the potholder (repeat potholder steps 1–5). Zigzag along the raw edges of the bib; then turn under ¼″ along 3 sides and stitch them down to hem 3 sides, leaving the bib bottom unhemmed.

11. For the waistband, cut 2 strips from red print fabric, 2½″ × 22″ each. Fold each strip in half crosswise to mark its center. Place the unhemmed edge of the bib at the center of one strip (see Figure 22–3a). Lay the second red print strip face-down over the bib. Stitch all along the edge, catching the apron bib in the stitching (see Fig. 22–3b). Turn and press the bands right-side out.

12. Take the apron skirt you set aside in Step 9. Mark the center of the apron skirt and the center of the waistband on the apron bib. Pin or baste the front layer of the waistband to the top of the apron skirt, matching centers; and pin the back layer of the waistband to the back of the apron. The waistband should extend ¼″ below the raw top edge of the apron skirt. Stitch the apron skirt to the waistband, and continue stitching beyond the apron skirt to close the rest of the waistband's long edge, but stop

gather top edge

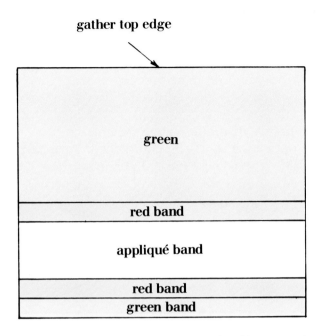

22–2 Construction diagram for the skirt part of the apron.

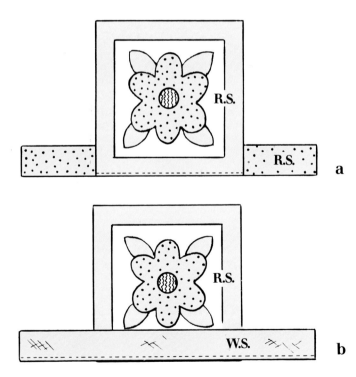

*22–3 Attaching the bib of the apron to the waistband. **a:** Attaching the first red strip. **b:** Attaching the second red strip over the bib and the first red strip. Dashed lines are stitching lines.*

stitching ¼″ before the short sides of the waistband.

13. For the waist ties, cut two 36″ × 4½″ strips from red print material. Fold each strip in half on its length, with the right sides of the fabric facing, and stitch along the open long edge and one short edge, leaving the remaining short edge unstitched. Turn each tie right-side out through the unstitched edge and press it. Turn under ¼″ at each end of the apron's waistband (see Fig. 22–4a, left). Insert the unstitched end of a waist tie into each open end of the waistband so that it is ½″ in, and pin it in place. Hand- or machine-stitch the tie to the waistband as shown in Figure 22–4a, close to the turned-in edge, to secure the ties.

14. For the neck ties, cut two strips, 2″ × 20″ each, from the red print material. With right sides of material facing in, fold them in half on their length and stitch each one closed along one long and one short side. Then turn the ties right-side out. Turn under the remaining raw edge on each one, and tack it in place on the wrong side of the top of the bib (see photo).

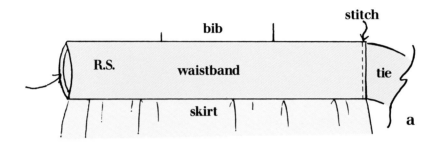

22–4 *Attaching the waist ties.* **a:** *Fold in ¼″ at the sides of the waistband (above, left). Insert the tie and stitch near the fold through the waistband and tie.* **b:** *One tie is attached to the waistband.*

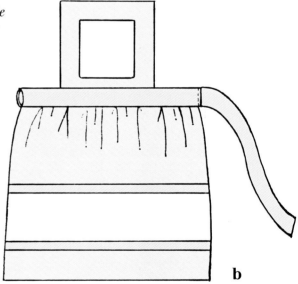

Index